MORNING, NOON AND NIGHT

*Prayers and meditations
mainly from
the Third World*

*Collected and introduced
by
John Carden*

Church Missionary Society
157 Waterloo Road, London SE1 8UU
1976

CHURCH MISSIONARY SOCIETY
© 1976

ISBN No. 900287 26 8

Printed by Bocardo & Church Army Press Ltd., Cowley, Oxford

CONTENTS

The dappled die-away
Cheek and the wimpled lip,
The gold-wisp, the airy-grey
Eye, all in fellowship—
This, all this beauty blooming,
This, all this freshness fuming,
Give God while worth consuming.

But thought and thew now bolder
And told by Nature: Tower;
Head, heart, hand, heel, and shoulder
That beat and breathe in power—
This pride of prime's enjoyment
Take as for tool, not toy meant
And hold at Christ's employment.

The vault and scope and schooling
And mastery in the mind,
In silk-ash kept from cooling,
And ripest under rind—
What life half lifts the latch of,
When hell stalks towards the snatch of,
Your offering, with despatch, of!

(Morning, Midday and Evening Sacrifice:
Gerard Manley Hopkins)

MORNING, NOON AND NIGHT

" It was on the eve of my departure that I heard the hidden message I was waiting for China to utter. I stood and watched our golden star as it sank below the dunes, taking with it the whole wide range of colour, and it seemed to me it was no longer the fiery sun I saw, but the very focus of terrestial life setting over the Mongolian desert to rise again *on us;* and from the whole of sleeping Asia I thought there rose a voice which whispered: ' Now, my brother of the West, *it is your turn. . . .*' Yes, sleep on ancient Asia, your people are weary, and your soil is ravaged. . . ." So wrote Teilhard de Chardin from Central Asia in a private letter dated October, 1932, and only a few years after Charles Perry Scott had composed his well-known prayer for the ill-fated Chung Hua Sheng Kung Hui, the Holy Catholic Church of China. Such words serve now as a memorial to our failure to act adequately when it *was* our turn.

These many sunset failures—when we tried either too much or too little—are, however, strongly counterbalanced in the popular Christian imagination by sentiments such as:

> As o'er each continent and island
> The dawn leads on another day
> The voice of prayer is never silent
> Nor dies the strain of praise away.

and by the grateful realisation that behind the euphoria of the well-known hymn there stands the solid fact of a Christian Church established now in almost every nation under the sun—and moon— and able, each part of it, to offer its own special brand of prayer and praise—and penitence.

Only too often, however, and in too many places, as the compilers of the report *Rural People at Worship* point out, there has been failure to earth the Christian faith in a meaningful manner, and the voice of prayer has too frequently been stilted and stylised. " Is there among you," the book asks, " any prophet, any statesman, any leader who will—as Moses once led the Israelites out of the Egyptian bondage—excite the human imagination and lead man back to nature, to sunlight, starlight, earth-breath, sweet air, beauty, gaiety and health ? "

That there *are* such praying men and women in the Third World will, I think, be evident from the prayers which follow, though many of them point to a different quality of freedom and a different kind of exodus from that envisaged by the writer. Certainly the symbol of the western exodus, the coca cola bottle, receives a hard knock in the prayer of the East Asia Youth Assembly: " O Lord, lead us not into imitation! "

In spite of the fact that the prayer for freedom has been answered in so many countries in the Third World—with an accompanying awakening of social and national awareness—the people of too many countries are still weary, and their soil irreparably ravaged. It is among such people and on such soil that the Church is established, and Christ is acknowledged.

" Finding God in the silences, we are uplifted in spirit," writes the author of a paper which appeared in the *Indian Witness*, " but the creaking of the cartwheels on the road outside recalls us to the fact that the Church of Christ in India has begun its day of toil. It is not a Church which has much time for silent meditation, but largely a Church which toils. In the forests, in the fields, on the dusty roads, in the schoolrooms, and in the humble homes, the Church of Christ in India is toiling." The writer then con- cludes: " Two ideals, then, we will put down in red letters for this toiling Church. First, that our form of worship must be adapted to the people and their needs. Second, that the people must be able to share in the worship. . . ."

What adaptation of worship and prayer may mean for a weary people in the awful Shinkawa slum of Kobe is suggested by Toyohiko Kagawa in a number of his prayers. At first reading these may seem to be somewhat alien to our experience. " There is naturally a difference," writes Kagawa, " in the religious temperament of the tropics and the religious experience of the temperate zone." The difference is readily distinguishable in a number of prayers in this book, and is reflected in the title of the poem: *Concerning the Difficulties of Faith in Hot Climates*, by the Muslim poet Shahid Hosain:

> If I must learn to praise
> And do obeisance in these barren wastes
> Hard prayers will grow upon a stony heart
> Flint striking flint, the sparks
> A pale and instant gleam under the sun. . . .

A number of prayers of this quality and with this kind of glint to them will be found in the following pages, composed mostly by godly Muslim men and women of prayer. Many more such prayers may be discovered in the collections made by Kenneth Cragg and Constance Padwick in their books *Alive to God: Muslim and Christian Prayer*, and *Muslim Devotions*.

That other forms of prayer from the Indian subcontinent need to be regarded in this kind of light and at this same temperature is suggested by Klaus Klostermeier in his exploration of the Christian presence in India, *Hindu and Christian in Vrindaban*, and specially in the chapter headed: *Theology at 120 °F*. " Theology," he says, and here he might also have included prayer and worship, " at 120 °F in the shade seems very different from the theology at 70 °F to which most of us western Christians have been accustomed by our upbringing." He continues: " The theologian at 120 °F sees the cracks in the soil and the world as a desert; he considers whether it would not be wiser to keep the last jug of water till the evening, he wishes the heat were a few degrees less, and he has to exert all his Christian faith trying to find a little bit of sense in his life wherein he plays such a very insignificant role, because he depends on so many people. . . ." Such prayers, therefore, are more suitable for use in a hot bath than in a cold church!

It is in spite of all this, and to all this, that Christians in the hot lands add, " through Jesus Christ our Lord ". For by and large, it is not the presence of so many people—what is often referred to as the humanisation issue—nor indeed the ever-present climate, but rather *Christ* himself who makes his unique impact on the prayer life of his people.

Some of the prayers and songs with which the Christians in the Third World greet and meet the events of each day and each changing circumstance in their lives, are contained in this book. They range from the experience in prison cell, to leprosy hospital; from concentration camp, to East African revival meeting. They include the prayer-poem of Toyohiko Kagawa written while in prison for leading a dock workers' strike and the meditation of an Indian Christian at dawn; they follow a lorry driver on the hazardous roads of West Africa, and the man missionary taking his first steps in love of a woman. They include those friends and neighbours among whom Christians live and work; the OM! of the pious Hindu, and the spontaneous prayer of the old Muslim man suddenly over-come by the diversity and solidarity of his own faith: O Lord, my Liege, unite us all; as well as the man from the Pacific who spends time quietly breathing breath into his prayers.

In an early and therefore important part of the book, are to be found the prayers of presence. The considerable number of prayers under this heading, and their special unhurried quality, suggest that only too often those of other cultures and faiths find it easier than do most of us to practise the presence of God and of another human being in this way. "And yet," says John Taylor in his book: *The Primal Vision*, on the Christian presence amid African religion, "the Christian, whoever he may be, who stands in the world in the name of Christ, has nothing to offer unless he offers to be present, really and totally present, really and totally in the present." "The failure of so many 'professional' Christians," he says, "is that only too often they are 'not all there'!"

Most of the prayers in this book are given special flavour and colour by their setting and by the relaxed presence of Christians in their own situation. A case in point is the songs and prayers of Narayan Vaman Tilak. "Until Tilak began to pour forth his bhajans," writes Father Jack Winslow, "it is hardly an exaggeration to say that Marathi-speaking Christians had no outlet for the pouring out of the heart's devotion in the worship of God. If music and hymn singing play no small part in a western service for the quickening of devotion and the offering of praise, in India their place is more central still. At the call of the guitar's twang and the cymbal's clash and the drum's rhythmic beat, the soul leaps up ready for the high emprise. As the familiar melody moves on and the voices expand into a great flood of sound, earth is left behind, its cares forgotten, its joys despised. The body sways rhythmically to the music; the spirit soars and sings at heaven's gate. The emotion changes with the mood of the music. Now it is the song of worship and adoration; now a passionate yearning for the Presence; now a transport of loving devotion; now the peace of calm self-surrender to the divine love. This to the Indian is worship, and from this the Indian Christian of Maharashtra was cut off till Tilak came. . . ."

The delight which present-day Persians take in the use of their language as a vehicle for the praise of Christ—even though, admittedly, it loses a lot in the process of translation—is strongly substantiated by their own much-treasured account of how the early Persian invaders spared the Basilica of the Nativity in Bethlehem only when they saw the picture of the Magi in *Persian* robes over the entrance.

Similarly, the sojourn of the Holy Family in Egypt is a matter of considerable pride for Christians in Egypt. It is

8

commemorated in a tradition of great hospitality, by the dedication to it of at least one church in Cairo, and is backed up by a considerable volume of devotion.

" Even in the midst of sordidness, dirt, stink, sickness, poverty, greed, natural calamity, dacoitry and the fear of it, shortage of essentials, inflation and our own tiredness and shortcomings, there is His beauty everywhere," write the little Bengali sisters of Christa Sevika Sangha, describing the scenario of their memorably simple prayer that at all times and in all places they may be responsive to the vision of God. " We find it in the brilliant starlit night, in the psychedelic sunset, in the stillness after a cyclone, in the sparkle in a child's eyes after he has had a good meal, or in the joy on the face of a woman who has earned money to feed her family or to buy a sari to cover her nakedness." It is thus that the prayers of God's people are finely clothed in Bangladesh.

No collection of prayers from or about the Third World would, of course, be complete without reference to the *Book of Common Prayer* and the manner in which its prayers have been adopted and assimilated and cherished by the churches of Africa and Asia, and the way in which the daily offices of Morning and Evening Prayer have become part and parcel of the devotional life of clergy and people. And so, writing of the Christians in his diocese in the Church of South India, the Bishop of Tirunelveli declares: " Twenty thousand people love their well-worn Anglican prayer book services well enough to attend often outwardly dull and formal services every day, sometimes twice a day." And adds, " This remarkable solidarity in worship cannot fail to be a way and a source of spiritual strength." While at the same time, and in a very different setting, and in a situation in which Christians are very few and very isolated, " It was while going up the Kina-batangan River," testifies the Chinese Bishop of Sabah, " in a small boat driven by an outboard motor, miles from anyone in the jungle, awed by the high tall trees of the jungle, that I found comfort in saying the daily offices of Morning and Evening Prayer, and felt the nearness of God, and the presence of the many people who were supporting me . . . and their prayer mingled with mine. . . ."

Directly or indirectly, the *Book of Common Prayer* has had an incalculable influence on the lives of countless Christians in the Third World. A great many of its prayers, of course, originated in the east, and have therefore returned to the Third World by a long and circuitous route. Others, regardless of origin, have succeeded in capturing the deep universal aspirations of men and women everywhere, and will continue to be used wherever Christians come together. For those with wide vision, the continual use of substantial parts of the *Book of Common Prayer* in so many countries throughout the world, must in itself suggest ways in which this can be exploited for good. And not only the thought-forms of the prayer book, but also the language has had a clearly detectable influence on Asian and African writers of prayer. Such prayers are perhaps easier for us western Christians to use and to understand than the Indian lyric, the Japanese haiku, or the Persian couplet, which reflect rather special local colour and religious interest; and yet, if persisted with, these too can lead the western Christian to a deeper understanding of his Third World brother or sister.

Other prayers which perhaps until recently were strange, particularly to Anglican ears, are those, which after the style of Michel Quoist, might be called 'intimacy prayers'. These are clearly designed for quiet reflection rather than for public use. One thinks particularly of *I Lie on my Mat and Pray*, and *I Sing Your Praise all the Day Long*, both of them collections of prayers by young West African Christians; *Prayers from an Island,* by Richard Wong of Hawaii; *Meditations of an Indian Christian,* by M. A. Thomas, and *The Cross is Lifted*, by Chandran Devanesen, and from which, as well as from other sources, an extensive selection of prayers has been taken. Many of these do not speak to our immediate need—why should they?—but they do put us into the habit of thinking and feeling in a manner which enables us to get inside another person's life. They enable us to put ourselves into the position of the man or the woman or the child in a particular situation, asking ourselves, for instance: if I were a lorry driver driving down that particular stretch of road, how would *I* feel? Or faced with that particular beggar's bowl, what would *my* response be? Of if *I* were a child in Uganda, living beside that particular expanse of water, with evening falling, how would I feel about the relevance of the education I was getting there for the life of the little family in the village back home? And how can any or all of this be linked with the ascription: ' through Jesus Christ my Lord '? In short, such so-called intimacy prayers provoke thought and comparison, and call hopefully for the exercise of our every God-given faculty for loving and understanding.

" Most Christians," says John Taylor somewhere, " spend most of their time giving themselves from the tops of their heads." As if to counter-balance this with a contribution uniquely their own and yet born out of a great deal of suffering and indignity, and after decades of being treated as if they were not all there, many of the prayers in this book are hot prayers; the prayers for freedom, for instance, or for those in need. It is easy in such prayers for us to hear again the voice of the Old Testament prophet complaining of God's treatment of his people, or, rather nearer our own time, the querulous tones of St. Theresa, " No wonder, God, you have so few friends if you treat them all like this! "

Similarly, the prayer for deliverance from the wrong kind of missionaries; or the prayer composed by Third World Christians in Bangkok: ' Lord, show us deeply how important it is to be useless,' hopefully, perhaps, that we western Christians would take the hint, and renounce a little of our innate activism in favour of more reflection and a little planned neglect!

" Sudden gushes of thought and feeling " is how, rather ideally, the familiar prayer book versicles and responses have been described. Perhaps some of the versicles and responses in this book emerging out of situations of great human need, blended with feeling, and linked to the thought of Christ, will succeed in touching more than the tops of our heads.

A number of prayers end in tears. Others are heavy with foreboding and anxiety. So that on the occasion of the sudden renewal of fighting in the Middle East, or the eruption of racial violence or communal hatred in some part of Africa or South Asia, we may find ourselves saying with some Asian Hal or African Falstaff, " I would it were bed time, Hal, and all well."

And so there are also night prayers, when the air is a little cooler perhaps, and the mood more composed. Some of the prayers in the second part of the book, as in the second part of a day, have a wistful ' would that it might be so ' quality to them, like the suggested Christian use of the prayers of other faiths; and like the inscription still found above the entrance of the Great Mosque of Damascus—a reminder of its earlier days—' Thy Kingdom, O Christ, is for all ages '.

Some prayers come from an earlier era of missionary endeavour and have a dated and slightly ironic twist to them. Some of the older prayers from Africa, for example, or the Charles Perry Scott prayer for the Holy Catholic Church in China. In the light of subsequent events, and seen by hindsight, these prayers now appear to be slightly ludicrous and pretentious. They pose the question: what went wrong? And were we not perhaps, even, praying for the wrong kind of things? In this respect, for instance, the very old Chinese prayer of Nestorian origin seems to have stood the test rather better. Why should this be? On the other hand, when one understands that Christianity in China today is very much a private affair, and its practice restricted to inner and largely unseen acts of praise and prayer, are those short prayers for Chinese Christian men and women written as long ago as the early 1900s really so hopelessly out of date as we might at first suppose? And is not all such self-questioning in the presence of God, followed by admission of failure and amendment of life, part and parcel of true prayer? We must surely be prepared to learn from our prayers of the past, and repent as much over our prayer as over our lack of it.

Other prayers in this collection—by contrast—have a strangely child-like quality to them. The prayers by young West African Christians, for instance, or the delightful request, ' make us like Queen Victoria ', of the children in Uganda, or the prayer of the new convert, Mustafah, the tailor. Prayers like these raise a lot of interesting questions, questions which New Testament scholars have long argued about in their interpretation, for instance, of parables such as the story of the unjust judge finally driven to action by the importunity of the widow! " The humour lies," says Don Cupitt (in his book *Christ and the Hiddenness of God)* " in the fact that it is religiously apt and fitting to command prayer to God in terms which are objectively obviously comical. . . ." and he continues, "So the tragi-comedy of theism is that the believer must take seriously at one level what he knows at another level to be comical. . . . And one of the tasks of theology is the seemingly prepostrous one of relating the relative, anthropomorphic deity of practical religion to the absolute, transcendent God." " Suddenly there is a point," says Thomas Merton in his *Asian Journals,* " when religion becomes laughable. Then you decide that you are *nevertheless* religious."

The prayers in this book, as you will see, are mostly very practical and down to earth, and do permit us a number of laughs in the presence of God at the truly comical things we human beings get up to. But they also combine this with a profound reverence and sense of the presence of God which, perhaps uniquely, so many Third World Christians are capable.

Under the title: *Morning, Noon and Night* these prayers attempt to bring together the many moods, aspirations and misgivings of a very large section of the human race, around the clock. But more immediately and profoundly, as the poem by Gerard Manley Hopkins most beautifully expresses it, they combine also to represent the morning, midday, and evening sacrifices asked of each one at different points in our lives. And at the end of the day, though we may smile to ourselves during the course of it, these are nevertheless not themes to be played with, but small serious sacrifices, little blood lettings, to be linked with the divine humanity of Christ, and offered to God:

> . . . as for tool, not toy meant
> And held at Christ's employment.

And this, certainly, was the intention of the many who prayed this book into being.

London.   John Carden.

References

Morning, Midday and Evening Sacrifice: Gerard Manley Hopkins. *The Poems of Gerard Manley Hopkins* edited by W. H. Gardner and N. H. Mackenzie, published by Oxford University Press by arrangement with the Society of Jesus.

Rural People at Worship, Agricultural Missions Inc. New York.

Paper in the *Indian Witness*, Florence Moyer Bollinger.

First Voices: Six Poets from Pakistan, Oxford University Press, Karachi.

Hindu and Christian in Vrindaban, Klaus Klostermaier, SCM.

The Primal Vision: Christian Presence amid African Religion, John V. Taylor, SCM.

Narayan Vaman Tilak: The Christian Poet of Maharashtra, J. C. Winslow, SCM, 1923.

Meditations by James Wong.

Apartheid and the Archbishop: Life and Times of Geoffrey Clayton, Alan Paton, Jonathan Cape.

The Asian Journal of Thomas Merton, Sheldon Press.

Christ and the Hiddenness of God: Don Cupitt, Lutterworth Press.

MORNING

Gandhiji had his devotions at four in the morning and then rested again until early dawn. There is naturally a difference in the religious discipline of the tropics and the religious experience of the temperate zone. We would do well, however, to copy India in our religious life.

After reposeful sleep, prayer in the early dawn, fellow-shipping with the morning star, brings to human beings the supremest of blessings. Jesus also loved the hours before the dawn. For ever let me be a child of the early dawn. . . .

Toyohiko Kagawa, Japan.

Sunrise is an event that calls forth solemn music in the very depths of man's nature, as if one's whole being had to attune itself to the cosmos and praise God for the new day, praise him in the name of all the creatures that ever were or ever will be. I look at the rising sun and feel that now upon me falls the responsibility of seeing what all my ancestors have seen, in the Stone Age and ever before it, praising God before me. Whether or not they praised him then, for themselves, they must praise him now in me. When the sun rises each one of us is summoned by the living and the dead to praise God.

Thomas Merton, Trappist monk, died Bangkok, 1968.

Thanks be to thee, O Lord, for this gift of a new day, which seemeth to me so like other days, yet is indeed not like but different. It is thy newest handiwork, the fruit of thy longest patience. Make it for me a time for service and a time for loving.

Prayer used by students of an Indian theological college.

O Thou
who hast given me eyes
to see the light
that fills my room,
give me the inward vision
to behold thee in this place.

O Thou
who hast made me to feel
the morning wind upon my limbs,
help me to feel thy Presence
as I bow in worship of thee.

Chandran Devanesen, India.

14

O God, Creator of Light: at the rising of your sun
this morning, let the greatest of all lights, your love,
rise like the sun within our hearts.

Prayer of the Armenian Apostolic Church.

Oh, shining morning, when I kneel to pray,
My loathsome, blinded body all forgot,
                        The door shut,
I, together with my thoughts,
Alone, amid the loveliness of dawn.

Prayer by Miyoshi, a Japanese leprosy patient.

What a fine morning! Lord, how lovely
Is this day that thou hast granted.

Meditation of an Indian Christian.

Receive the thanksgiving of a grateful people, O God, for
the light of another Hawaiian sunrise, for work that calls up
the best in us, and for the deep surmise that it is from thee
that we first knew the love of all peoples. Amen.

Richard Wong, Hawaii.

O God, who sends the light to shine upon this earth;
God, who makes the sun shine upon those who are good
and those who do wrong; God, who created the light that
lights the whole world, shine your light into our minds and
our hearts. Guard us from all that is harmful to ourselves
and others.

Prayer of the Egyptian Coptic Church.

O God, give me strength to live another day. Let me not
turn coward before its difficulties, or prove recreant to its
duties. Let me not lose faith in my fellow-men, keep me
sweet and sound of heart, in spite of ingratitude, treachery
and meanness. Preserve me from minding little stings or
giving them. Help me to keep my heart clean, and live so
honestly and fearlessly that no coward failure can dis-
hearten me or take away the joys of conscious integrity.
Open wide the eyes of my soul that I may see good in all
things. Grant me this day some new vision of thyself,
inspire me with thy spirit of joy and gladness, and make
me the cup of strength to suffering souls in the Name of the
strong Deliverer, our only Lord and Saviour Jesus Christ.
Amen.

A prayer of Bishop Kimber Den of Chekiang,
and which he used daily in prison.

We thank thee, our king, for a new day,
For a new pouring forth of thy wine of life,
For a new bidding to thy feast,
To the eternal triumph-banquet of thy kingdom,
Wherein we on earth and thy beloved in heaven,
May conjointly be glad and rejoice,
Sharing the divine revelry,
The melody, the rapture of perfect delight.

Give us, we pray thee, the simplicity and purity of little
children,
That, nothing questioning, we may gather gladly,
With thy whole family in heaven and earth,
Round this thy table of a new day.
Make thin, O Lord, make very thin the veil
Which divideth us who are yet in the flesh
From those others, our fellow-guests,
Who feast with us, unseen by our outward eyes,
But to be beheld how wondrously,
In what clear glory of deathless perfection,
When thou dost enlighten the eyes of our spirit,
With the eternal radiance of thine own presence.

For fitness to be guests at God's banquet:
a prayer written for use in an Indian college.

What joy it is at early morn to meet
Beside the sea, with those who love our Lord
And whom we love; and there to read the Word,
And lay our burdens at our Master's feet.

Prayer of Nagata, a Japanese leprosy patient·

O God, whose patience is beyond the longest day, grant
me today, eagerness to do my work,
curiosity to push into the new,
determination to verify rumour,
and courage to live until sundown. Amen.

Prayer from Hawaii.

This day will I praise thee, O Lord:
This day will I thank thee, O Lord:
This day will I love thee, O Lord:
This day will I serve thee, O Lord.

Prayer suggested for use by an Indian theological college.

Rise, rise, oh my Soul
Praise the Lord of Day and Night
In the beginning of the new path of Life
Sing the glory of God.

Morning song used every day by the Marathi
Christian poet Narayan Vaman Tilak.

16

I have been always looking to the future for opportunities to glorify thee. I live in the future and not in this day that thou hast made. A life of dedication I want to have, but I am longing to have it only in the future. I want to make my relations pure only in the future. I am a Christian, in a dream, living in an unreal future world, neglecting the marvellous opportunities thou offerest me today. Lord, give me the strength to rise above the weakness of 'postponement' and continuously create in me a feeling of 'life is today', for tomorrow I may never be.

Meditation of an Indian Christian.

God knoweth best what is needful for us,
And all that he does is for our good.

Prayer used by the Companions of
Brother Lawrence, India.

Lord Jesus, so real, so near, so dear
   To all whom I love
   To all whom I meet
   To all for whom I pray
Be real, be near, be dear today,
   increasingly, for ever.

A prayer sometimes used by members of the
Christa Mahila Sadan, Women's Centre, North India.

PRAYERS OF PRESENCE

A friend of mine, a Japanese missionary in Thailand, has among his acquaintances a few deeply religious Buddhist monks. On one occasion they decided to enter into theological discussion, and as part of the process resolved to study together their respective scriptures. One of the books they chose was St. John's Gospel. So, one day, they began the study of John, and started with the first verse of the first chapter, " In the beginning was the Word." " My," said one of the Buddhist monks, " even in the beginning you Christians didn't have a little time for silence! "
There is no doubt about it that those of other faiths often find us Christians a noisy and boisterous people, with no great depth to us, and little time for quiet.

T. K. Thomas, South Indian editorial secretary
of the Christian Literature Society of Madras.

" Before the missionaries came, my people used to sit outside their temples for a long time meditating and preparing themselves before entering. Then they would virtually creep to the altar and offer their petition and afterwards would again sit a long time outside, this time— as they put it—to ' breathe life ' into their prayers. The Christians, when they came, just got up, uttered a few sentences, said Amen and were done. For that reason my people called them Haolis—' without breath ', meaning, those who failed to breathe life into their prayers."

Tales of the South Pacific: James Michener.

Lord, I just don't know what to say when I am asked to make a prayer. It is like being asked to breathe.

Young Indian Christian participant in School
on Worship: South India.

Oh, make my heart so still, so still,
                When I am deep in prayer,
That I may hear the white mist-wreaths
                losing themselves in air.

Utsunomiya: a Japanese leprosy patient.

Send down, O God, O Gentle and Compassionate One,
into my heart faith and tranquillity and stillness, that I may
be one of those whose hearts are tranquillised by the
mention of God.   *Ibn-al-Arabi.*

Create, O God, thy temple upon earth
Everlasting God, create it presently,
Create it now.   *Well-known Jewish prayer.*

O Thou, great beyond imagination, or measure, or thought,
or conjecture; beyond all that has been spoken, or heard,
or read; we are still at the commencement only of our
acknowledgement of thy attributes.

Sa'adi, Persian poet, 15th century.

Thou art the Great God—he who is in heaven.
Thou art the Creator of life, thou makest the regions above.
Thou art the Hunter who hunts for souls.
Thou art the Leader who goes before us.
Thou art the great Mantle which covers us.
Thou art he whose hands are with wounds.
Thou art he whose feet are with wounds.
Thou art he whose blood is a trickling stream.
Thou art he whose blood was spilled for us.
Thou art the Great God.

Prayer of a Xhosa Christian.

Let my soul be a mirror that will reflect thee to the world.
Live thou in my thought.
Live thou in my speech.
Live thou in all my deeds
O most Holy.

Prayer of Narayan Vaman Tilak,
Marathi Christian poet.

Holy God.
Holy and Mighty, Holy and Immortal, have mercy on us.
Holy God.
Holy and Mighty, Holy and Immortal, have mercy on us.
Holy God.
Holy and Mighty, Holy and Immortal, have mercy on us.

The Trisagion, taken from Holy Qurbana of the
Syrian Churches of Malabar, and included in the
Liturgy of the Church of South India.

We reverently worship
   the mysterious Person, God the Father;
   the responding Person, God the Son;
   and the witnessing Person, the spirit of Holiness.
We worship the Holy Trinity
Three persons in one.

Chinese Trinitarian formula used in the
worship of the Nestorian Church.

Reveal thyself to me, reveal thyself to me.
I seek not wealth nor power, I yearn to see thee alone.
O God, I care not for renunciation or enjoyment, I yearn
   to see thee alone.
O God, I am neither anxious for home, nor for the forest
   life;

I only yearn to see thee.
Yea I seek for naught save thee, O God, I yearn for
   thy vision alone; grant my prayer.
                    Dadu: 16th century Hindu poet and mystic.

O God, our hearts are homesick until they rest in thee, for
thou hast made them for thyself.
                    St. Augustine of Hippo.

" If I ask him for a gift, he will give it to me, and then I
shall have to go away. But I don't want to go away.
Give me no gift—give me thyself. I want to be with thee,
my beloved."
                    *Prayer ascribed to the oral tradition of
                    a hill tribe in Northern Bengal.*

Thou my mother, and my father thou.
Thou my friend, and my teacher thou.
Thou my wisdom, and my riches thou.
Thou art all to me, O God of all gods.
                    Ramanuja.

I pray not for wealth, I pray not for honours, I pray not for
pleasures, or even the joys of poetry. I only pray that during
all my life I may have love: that I may have pure love
to love Thee.
                    Chaitanya, the Indian mystic AD 1500.

O God, here we are, all devoted to thee;
   make us according to thy heart.
                    Prayers of the Companions of Brother Lawrence, India.

Jesus, I wish I were a poet,
My mind sings and my heart leaps,
Thoughts of joy arise from my bosom,
And a note of gratefulness is all about me;
All, at the very thought of thee,
Who art my dearest;
For thy love and divine mercy,
And for thyself—
O I want to sing praises to thee,
For thou art the end of my life.

I would make a garland with jasmine flowers
And watch thee wearing it for me.
I would look at thee from foot to head, and enjoy thy love;
But who am I to dare to make a gift to thee?
Lord, Lord of my life, forgive my foolish words;
Take my life, O Lord, and weave a garland for thyself.
                    A garland: meditation by an Indian Christian.

PRAYERS OF NEED

A diet of tears is not savoury. O spirit of Midnight,
collect thou my tears in the bamboo tube. As my mass
before God I will bring the tears of melancholy. I have now
nothing else to offer on God's altar. Instead of the oil of
the festival season I will bring before God my bamboo
tube of tears. In it are stored tears of repentance, tears of
gratitude for favours granted, tears in acknowledgement
of blessings received, tears which flowed when emotions
ran high, and tears of ecstasy. Created a child of tears,
I am ashamed to advance into God's presence in the full
light of day. Alone, in secret, in the midnight hour I seek
his face.

Melt, O pupil of my eyes! Let their very lenses stream
forth. Shall I not offer up to God the very marrow of my
soul? I yearn that these tears for the altar shall emit the
sweetest fragrance. I want them to be as clear as crystal.

Tears! O tears! Tears wrung out of the soul's very
marrow. Tears of ecstasy in drawing nigh to God! Tears
of horror in not being able to enter into his presence.
Tears which cause a plaintive melody as they alternate
and intermingle! Come, O tears! Come without
hesitation before God.

Toyohiko Kagawa, Japan.

I am glad, Lord, for I wept today,
And I hid my tears inside my handkerchief.
Still my eyes were burning, and my head got hot;
My heart was beating fast and I felt weak,
Solemn thoughts rose up from my mind,
And a note of thankfulness played its melody in my being.
Why? I do not know.
I know that drops of tears which I hid in my kerchief,
Have been a stepping stone for me to thee,
Lord, I cry, make me weep,
And give me tears to flow;
Thy loving touch transforms my grief
Into joy, and peace, and I weep in love—
I am glad, Lord, for I wept to day.

I weep in love: meditation by an Indian Christian.

I have no other helper than you, no other father, I pray
   to you.
Only you can help me. My present misery is too great.
Despair grips me, and I am at my wit's end.
O Lord, Creator, Ruler of the World, Father,
I thank you that you have brought me through.
How strong the pain was—but you were stronger.
How deep the fall was—but you were even deeper.
How dark the night was—but you were the noonday
   sun in it.
You are our father, our mother, our brother, and our friend.

An African's prayer.

O precious love, of my redemption part,
Ever the more unfolding with its warmth
The ice-cold weariness of my poor heart.

Yamagata: a Japanese leprosy patient.

My Lord God, my All in all, Life of my life, and Spirit of
my spirit, look in mercy upon me and so fill me with thy
Holy Spirit that my heart shall have no room for love of
aught but thee.

I seek from thee no other gift but thyself, who art the
giver of life and all its blessings. From thee I ask not for
the world or its treasures, nor yet for heaven even make
request, but thee alone do I desire and long for, and where
thou art, there is heaven. The hunger and the thirst of this
heart of mine can be satisfied only with thee who hast
given it birth.

O Creator mine! Thou hast created my heart for thyself
alone, and not for another, therefore this my heart can find
no rest or ease save in thee; in thee who hast both
created it and set in it this very longing for rest. Take
away then from my heart all that is opposed to thee, and
enter and abide and rule for ever. Amen.

Sadhu Sundar Singh, of North India:
prayed in the jungle when he repelled the
tempter, then beheld his Saviour.

Lord, we know not what is good for us. Thou knowest
what it is. For it we pray. Amen.

Prayer used by the Khonds in North India.

22

O my God,
If I worship thee in desire for heaven,
    exclude me from heaven;
If I worship thee for fear of hell,
    burn me in hell.
But if I worship thee for thyself alone,
    then withhold not from me thine eternal beauty.
> *Rabia, a Muslim woman mystic of Basrah and*
> *Jerusalem about AD 800.*

O God, have mercy on this man so full of sin. Truly pity
me. I know that there is nothing real except that which is
related to thee. Truly pity me, and support this slight
work of mine. Please hear this prayer in the name of
Jesus Christ. Amen.
> *Prayer of a Japanese Christian novelist and seeker.*

O God, I ask of thee a perfect faith, a sincere assurance, a
reverent heart, a remembering tongue, a good conduct of
commendation, and a true repentance, repentance before
death, rest at death, and forgiveness and mercy after death,
clemency at the reckoning, victory in paradise and escape
from the fire, by thy mercy, O mighty one, O Forgiver,
Lord increase me in knowledge and join me unto good.
> *A Muslim prayer, used after the Muslim pilgrim to*
> *Mecca has begun the seventh circuit of the Kabah.*

I remember with shame my failures and sins, Lord. I
realise that my private sins are injuries to the world-wide
Christ-body here on earth, a grievance to the saintly and
angelic communion there in heaven, and a recrucifixion of
thee, my Saviour. Pardon me, forgive me, cleanse me and
restore into my soul divine spotlessness and godliness.

God whose glory is most glorious, whose love most
loving, whose might most mighty, whose holiness most
holy, whose peace most peace-giving, we praise thee
and adore thy splendour. Our thankful hearts we lay open
before thee, asking that thou wilt accept our thanks and
adoration through the same our Saviour, Jesus Christ.
> *Prayers of a Kenyan Christian.*

Tukutendereza Yesu,	Glory, glory, Hallelujah
Yesu Omwana gw' endiga,	Glory, glory to the Lamb
Omusaigwo gunasiza,	For the cleansing blood has
Nkwebaza Omulokozi.	reached me,
	Glory, glory to the Lamb.

> *Tukutendereza: Prayer of forgiveness and praise in Luganda*
> *used continually by Balokeli Christians in East Africa.*

O God, we hope in you
   that you will help us in all our troubles
   that you will strengthen us in all our temptations
   that you will forgive us all our sins
   that you will be with us when we die
      and be merciful to us when we are judged:

O God in you have we trusted, let us never be confounded.
     Prayer often used in Lent in many Nigerian churches.

Lord of truth and of mercy, we pray thee to take away
   our selfishness and give us thy holiness;
   our indifference and give us thy zeal;
   our smallness and make us generous;
   our thirst for recognition and make us thirst for
     righteousness.
       Prayer of United Church of North India.

O God, fan to a flame in me, and in thy Church, the fire
of thy life which has burnt low. Amen.
       Prayer used in the Diocese of Krishna-Godavari,
           Church of South India.

O thou to whom we always look,
   lighten our hearts
   as the sun throws light
   upon the dark bushes around us.
May we always reflect thy radiance
   so that those who have not known thee
   may see thee in us.
In the name of the Great Light we ask this.
       Prayer of an African Christian teacher.

Lord, make this world to last as long as possible.
      Prayer of 11-year-old child on hearing
       of Sino-Indian border fighting.

O Lord, we beseech thee to deliver us from the fear of the
unknown future; from fear of failure; from fear of poverty;
from fear of bereavement; from fear of loneliness; from
fear of sickness and pain; from fear of age; and from fear
of death. Help us, O Father, by thy grace to love and
fear thee only, fill our hearts with cheerful courage and
loving trust in thee; through our Lord and Master Jesus
Christ.
       Akanu Ibiam: Nigeria.

Thou art our need and to thee we come, a song of
thanksgiving in our hearts sweeter than the song of
harvesting women, more eternal than the earth. For thy
gifts are of thee, and thou art God, thou art Creator, thou
art Giver, thou art Father, *thou art our need*.

Give us strength to multiply our love as a grain of rice
multiplies its seed, as the rivers spread throughout the
land, as the sound of drums reaches mountain crests.
Give us strength to open our arms to those who hate us,
to embrace thy Son's ' seventy times seven ', to make the
words of our mouth as gentle as our Lord's ' Peace be
unto you ', to see no colour but thy forgiveness. O God
thou art our need.

From thy immeasurable love send the rain to our fields,
send the sun and gentle it, give sweetness to the hands of
those who make our harvesting tools, shield our fruit-
bearing trees from barrenness, steady our bodies and make
keen our eyes as we stalk game in the forest. Make our
work in village and city, in field and office, fruitful to
others and to ourselves and in thy sight.

O God, *thou art our need*. Strip fear from us as the
hunter strips skin from his game. Let us in nothing be
anxious. Let our courage be as steady as the giant
cottonwood, as penetrating as the harmattan wind, as
contagious as a child's laugh, for *thou art our need*.

Prayer from Africa.

O God of goodness,
in the mystery of natural disasters we look to thee,
trusting that there is an explanation that will
satisfy our minds and hearts.
Accept our compassion for our fellow-men,
our desire for their relief,
and our hope for knowledge which shall control
the forces of nature.
Help us to help thee complete thy universe,
O Creator Father,
to remove its flaws,
so that we may be sub-creators with thee of the
Kingdom of thy love in Jesus Christ.

Prayer on learning of disastrous floods in
Bangladesh.

Help us, O Lord, bear that which we cannot bear.

Inscription on the tomb of Mumtaz Mahal wife of
Shah Jahan, Agra.

O God
you can make it tough,
but please,
don't make it
impossible!
Prayer of Uruguayan survivors of plane crash in the Andes.

*Letter from a Pakistani Muslim Girl Student
following the loss of Bangladesh:*

Dear God,

You don't seem to be around very much and I am so
alone and lonely that I am beginning to miss you—a little.
Do you think it would be asking too much for you to come
back again? It isn't such a difficult thing to do. I should
like to talk to you about so many things. I know you
don't answer but even then it is nice just to talk to you
hoping that you might be listening. There are chances that
you might be even somewhat interested in what I have
to say. Besides you don't get bored easily—do you?

Some people around here think you're awful, hard and
uncompromising. I think so too at times and it is true.
But I see what other people don't see—your unique sense
of humour. Take my mother, for instance. Most of the
time she lives in terrible fear of you. By her own confession
her actions are a result of an angry and harsh God, not a
loving God. There are others who are constantly warning
me to beware of your terrible wrath. I would sue them in
court for libel if I could but I am as yet a minor and the
courts around here are no good anyway. Actually it's
you who's being maligned and since there is no higher
court of appeal than yours, I suppose you will just have to
bear it—or lump it, as the Americans say. Anyway most
of the time when people think you're busy being angry and
terrible, I get the impression you're rolling with laughter
on the floors of Paradise. But, God, if you don't have a
sense of humour, please develop one fast because otherwise
you will become very uninteresting and I shall become
lonelier still. Besides my life depends on your sense of
humour, since I've been going through it hoping you will
laugh rather than frown. I don't want to come to the end
of the road to find an angry unpleasant and foreign God
while all the while I am hoping you're great fun—at times.

I know lately I have hated you. Nights I raged against you
but with an impotent fury. But please admit that you have
been very far away—so far away that I couldn't reach you.
I saw you take away the lovely land you gave to me and
I hated you. People suffered, they bled and cried out but

26

you were not moved. I called out to you—sleeping and waking. Apparently you chose not to hear. I remember as though it was now that afternoon in December. It had rained all day. The sky was bleak, the rooms depressingly dark. As I stood looking out of the window at the constantly falling rain, at the naked twisted branches stretching out towards you as if in some terrible agony— I wept and whispered your name over and over again. And while the tears fell, I thought as one does so strangely of insignificant things at moments of great anguish, of the last time I had cried as a child of nine. I never did let myself cry for I thought it was a sign of self-pity and weakness.

And yet watching the grey rain fall I felt, in my bewildered imagination, as if it fell on my hopes, my dreams weeping them away. God, how I hated you.

That afternoon is many, many months in the past. That sentimentality is dead again. But my search for you is on. I became very lonely when I snapped diplomatic ties with you because then, although I knew you were around somewhere, I couldn't or wouldn't say hullo to you. And I went to bed without talking to you. God, you wouldn't know what it feels like when suddenly there is a failure to communicate—specially since *you* haven't ever gone to bed and haven't had any God of your own. It was a childish thing to do, it was a silly thing to do, but it seemed the only thing that I could do then.

And if you haven't understood by now, that all this time I have been trying to apologise, then you're a more obstinate God than I thought you would be. Please come back. I tried doing without you, but now I've got into the habit of having you around and find it difficult to manage. I would try to get over the habit, but I'm not too good at that sort of thing. Besides, being an atheist is no longer very fashionable—neither is it very original. There are too many of them littering the streets. I for one definitely do not want to land in a garbage heap and rot. Moreover you don't want to be by-passed. So, God, let us call a halt to our cold war. In any case this is a time of rapprochement in certain smug quarters of the world. Why can't a truce be signed between God and a very presumptuous mortal?

And now I am very sleepy so that I cannot go on saying I am sorry. In a minute I shall be falling off to sleep—please don't let me have any nightmares.

Hoping to have you with me,
Yours ever,

PRAYERS OF LIFE AND WORK

Let us present our offerings to the Lord with reverence and godly fear:

Prayer Book of the Church of India, Pakistan, Burma and Ceylon.

For village life:

O God, help us to be thy instruments through whom thy will may be done in our village as in heaven.

Poverty, disease, ignorance, selfishness, strife, immorality, caste and untouchability are not according to thy will for our village. Help us to submit ourselves to thy will, that others may submit themselves to bring spiritual regeneration, economic prosperity and community goodwill to all our villages.

In all our personal undertakings and public dealings with men, in all our daily occupations, whether it be ploughing in the field, or running a boat, keeping the home for the family or buying provisions in the weekly market, tanning a hide or making a rope, building a house or cutting a drain, may we accept thy kingship over all our life and perform all our work under thy constant ruling eye. So may thy will be done in our village as in heaven.

Medak Diocese, Church of South India.

Seed we bring
Lord, to Thee, wilt Thou bless them, O Lord!
Gardens we bring
Lord, to Thee, wilt Thou bless them, O Lord!
Hoes we bring
Lord, to Thee, wilt Thou bless them, O Lord!
Knives we bring
Lord, to Thee, wilt Thou bless them, O Lord!
Hands we bring
Lord, to Thee, wilt Thou bless them, O Lord!
Ourselves we bring
Lord, to Thee, wilt Thou bless them, O Lord!

East African hymn used at Seed Consecration Service.

O God, who sendest the rains and fruitful seasons, who
visitest the earth and waterest it, we thy servants give thee
humble and grateful thanks for this new harvest season.
For bountiful crops and a fruitful season we give thee our
offering of praise. Thou hast crowned this year with thy
goodness.

We dedicate now this threshing floor to thee. May all the
grain threshed here be used for thy glory alone. May thine
angels guard this place, and these thy servants who shall
here thresh the grain thou gavest. Grant that of this
precious grain, none may be lost, but that it shall all be
used to feed thy hungry children. May all who eat it know
that of thy grace and love thou givest them bread in due
season. May even the little birds who shall glean their
food here be conscious of the heavenly father's care.
Through Jesus Christ our Lord, who is the true Bread of
Life come down from heaven. Amen.

Prayer used by many Indian Christian farmers at
dedication of a threshing floor.

Prayer for poor labouring folk:

Humbly, simply, we come early, praise God's kindness, his
great mercy.
Beg him pity our distress, grant forgiveness for each
trespass.
Bitter each day is our labour.
As we worship in this temple, fill our souls with his great
peace.
Now we know God's grace will never cease.
Sometimes we bear pain and suffering till our hearts are full
of darkness.
Father, never from us depart, keep us poor folk in your kind
heart.
God, give grace to us and gladness, bring us joy despite
our sadness.
May your mercy be our stay, may your love enlighten each
day.

Chao Tzu-Ch'en 1931: China.

As tools come to be sharpened by the blacksmith, so may
we *come,* O Lord. As sharpened tools go back with their
owner, so may we *go* back to our everyday life and work, to
be used by thee, O Lord.

A prayer of Zande Christians to whom the local
blacksmith would be a familiar sight.

For palm-oil and coconut industries:

We pray thee, O God, for thy blessing on the Palm Oil and Coconut industries; upon the palm trees and their fruits; upon those who climb the trees that their ropes may be strong; upon those who gather and those who carry; upon those who manufacture and those who use the products; that all men may use these gifts for the benefit of their fellow-men.

Rogationtide prayer; Niger and Niger Delta Dioceses—Occasional Services.

For the market:

O God our Father, we pray thee to bless this market and all who buy and sell in it. Be with the traders also as they travel from place to place. Protect them and us in body and soul. Help us to deal honestly and fairly with one another so that everyone may benefit from the trade that is done, and live together in peace and prosperity, giving thee thanks for all thy gifts. We ask it for the sake of Jesus Christ our Lord.

Rogationtide Service, Book of Occasional Services, Niger and Niger Delta Dioceses.

Lord,
the motor under me is running hot.
Lord,
there are twenty-eight people
and lots of luggage on the truck.
Underneath are my bad tyres.
The brakes are unreliable.
Unfortunately I have no money,
and parts are difficult to get.

Lord,
I did not overload the truck.
Lord,
' Jesus is mine '
is written on the vehicle,
for without Him I would not drive
a single mile.
The people in the back are relying on me.
They trust me because they see the words:
' Jesus is mine '.
Lord,
I trust You!

First comes the straight road
with little danger,
I can keep my eyes on the women,

children and chickens in the village.
But soon the road begins to turn,
it goes up and down,
it jumps and dances,
this death-road to Kumasi.
Tractors carrying mahogany trunks drive
as if there were no right or left.
Lord,
Kumasi is the temptation
to take more people than we should.
Let's overcome it!

The road to Accra is another problem.
Truck drivers try to beat the record,
although the road is poor
and has many holes
and there are many curves
before we come to the hills.

And finally to Akwapim.
Passing large churches in every village,
I am reminded of You, and in reverence
I take off my hat.
Now downhill in second gear.
One more temptation;
the straight road to Accra.
Lord, keep my feet steady on the pedals
even on the straight road to Accra.

Lord,
I sing hallelujah
when the ride is ended,
for You brought the truck and the people
in safety
through the hustle and bustle of Accra.

Lord, all is mercy,
because
' Jesus is mine '.
Hallelujah.
Amen.

Truck driver's prayer by a young Ghanaian
Christian.

Prayer when opening door:
I pray thee, Lord, to open the door of my heart to receive
thee within my heart.
When washing clothes:
I pray thee, Lord, to wash my heart, making me white as
snow.

When sweeping floors:
I pray thee, Lord, to sweep away my heart's uncleanness,
that my heart may always be pure.
When pouring oil:
I pray thee, Lord, to give me wisdom like the wise virgins
who always had oil in their vessels.
When posting a letter:
I pray thee, Lord, to add to me faith upon faith, that I may
always have communication with thee.
When drawing water:
I pray thee, Lord, to give me living water, that I may never thirst.
When lighting lamps:
I pray thee, Lord, to make my deeds excellent like lamps
before others, and more, to place thy true light within my heart.
When watering flowers:
I pray thee, Lord, to send down spiritual rain into my heart,
to germinate the good seed there.
When boiling water for tea:
I pray thee, Lord, to send down spiritual fire to burn away
the coldness of my heart and that I may always be hot-
hearted in serving thee.

> *Prayers for Chinese Christian women.*

For the river:
Protect, O Lord, we beseech thee, all those who fish in the
rivers and creeks of this country.   Give strength to their
arms as they paddle their canoes and cast their nets.
Grant them success in their work.   In the anxious hours of
waiting, steady and support them, and grant them in
dangers often, in watching often, in weariness often, they
may have a quiet mind; through Jesus Christ our Lord.

> *Service for the Blessing of Canoes and*
> *Nets, Book of Occasional Services,*
> *Niger and Niger Delta Dioceses.*

Almighty God, we have come together to praise and to
   thank you:
For our lives, our health and well being.
   Thank you very much O Lord!
For the factories that give us work and our daily bread.
   Thank you very much O Lord!
For our friends in and outside our work-place.
   Thank you very much O Lord!
For Jesus Christ who died for us that we might live.
   Thank you very much O Lord!
For the fact that you are our loving father who cares for us all.
   Thank you very much O Lord!

> *Prayer used at Industrial Thanksgiving Service,*
> *Jinja Industrial Mission, Uganda.*

On building a wall:
I pray thee, Lord, to make my faith as firmly established as a house built upon a rock, so that neither rain, flood nor wind can ever destroy it.

On pruning a tree:
I pray thee, Lord, to purge me and take away my selfishness and sinful thoughts, that I may bring forth more fruits of the Spirit.

On tending sheep:
I pray thee, Lord, to protect me from evil and keep me from want, daily carrying me in thine arms like a lamb.

On winnowing grain:
I pray thee, Lord, to winnow away the chaff from my heart and make it like the true wheat, fit to be garnered in thy barn.

On weeding the ground:
I pray thee, Lord, to take away the grass and weeds from my heart, and make truth spring up in my heart as the grain in the fields grows daily.

On sowing seed:
I pray thee, Lord, to sow the good seed of virtue in my heart, letting it grow day and night and bring forth a hundredfold.

On writing in a book:
I pray thee, Lord, by the precious blood of Jesus, to pay my debt of sin and to write my name in heaven, making me free in body and soul.

On planing wood:
I pray thee, Lord, to make me smooth and straight, fit to be a useful vessel, pleasing to the Lord.

On drawing water:
I pray thee, Lord, to give living water to quench my thirst, and wash away the stains from my heart.
                    Prayers for Chinese Christian men.

We thank thee, God, for the moments of fulfilment:
the end of a day's work,
the harvest of sugar cane,
the birth of a child,
for in these pauses, we feel the rhythm of the eternal. Amen.
                    Prayer from Hawaii.

O father give me passport
O mother give me passport
Elder brother give me passport
To job and life
Give me education.

Father, I'm really tired
Of looking after goats
I'm exhausted
I cannot chase anymore
Your wild cow
While my friends go to school
to obtain their passports.

Father, please I beg you
Don't be mad with me
Sell the goats
Sell the cows
Sell everything
And give me all the money
To pay for my passport
To job and life
Give me education
I pray you.

Give me life
Give me respect not of a porter
Give me sonhood
Give me education
The international passport to living
And I'll give you fatherhood.

Father if you deny me passport
You deny me life and fatherhood.
And blame yourself for murder;
Let me live I pray you
If you're really my father.

Prayer/poem of Ugandan Christian.

O Almighty God, Father of all beings, Creator of the seas,
mountains and things that move and are movable, here we
give our thanks at the thought of naming this House, *Falls
House.* O God, we pray that this House may be given thy
blessings at all times and may the power of thy Son lead
thy children to the way of understanding more of thy work
now and always.

*Written in English by Junior School girls of
Wanyange Girls' School, Jinja, Uganda, and one
of a number commemorating famous names and places.*

O God, we thank thee for work done to thy little children, play and all beautiful things that please our life here. And here we glorify thy holy name at this time of giving this House the name of *Nile House*, and at remembering the great river Nile and its meaning for us. Bless this House and the children who sleep in it, for the love of thy only Son Jesus Christ.

Written in English by primary children and their housemistress.

Lord, we thank you for all the lakes which you have given us in the world, in which are most sufficient things which you put inside them, such as food we eat which comes from the lakes and is very useful for our bodies. And it is so deep and calm, and people use it for their journeys and travel across it to other countries and make their journey much shorter. We also get the most important drink of water and also use it for cooking, bathing, washing and other things which need water. So we also ask you to make our house as useful as the lake's uses, and make it important. Through Jesus Christ our Lord. Amen.

Written in English by the girls themselves.

O God our Father, Almighty Ruler of all, we thank thee for the good things thou hast done for us in this House in giving us this name *River* which is new to us and reminds us that every created thing rejoices because of the goodness of rivers. Help us, O Lord, to do good, to be well behaved and obedient, and that each thing that we do may glorify the goodness of thy name, be of value in our lives, and bring us to everlasting life, through the mercy of thine only Son Jesus Christ our Lord.

Written in Luganda, by primary children.

O God, our Father, we thank thee, we praise thee, for the lovely name you have chosen through other people for our House. Make this House as strong as Queen Victoria herself was. Make it as brave as she was. Give its house prefects and all its members wisdom to build it up. Help its house prefects to develop a quality of leadership like Queen Victoria. Through the merits of Jesus Christ our Lord.

Written in English by the girls and their housemistress.

O God, we thank you for giving us the chance of living in this new and well-built house on this beautiful hill. We thank you for the River Nile and for the power of the Owen Falls which turns the machines which make electricity. As we live in this House, may we sometimes think of Owen and all the other brave men who helped this country to go forward. Let us follow in their way, so that many good things may come to this country of ours. Help us to remember that a dormitory and a school are not made by beautiful buildings, but by all the people who live in them. Help us to live in this House happily. Let us work together, in this little part of Africa, so that we may make the whole of Africa a happy part of your kingdom. Bless and keep us all in *Owen House.*

Written in English by Junior Secondary Girls and their English housemistress.

Lord
we thank you
that we may attend
this good and expensive school.
We thank you for every day.
Lord
we thank you for this day.
Our bodies grow stronger
from the good food.
Our minds are sharpened,
numbers, dates
and phrases are being remembered.
Lord,
did I also come closer to you?

Lord,
tonight I remember my parents,
my brothers and sisters.
My day was easy.
My arms are not swollen,
my back does not hurt.
Lord,
I was sitting on a stool
while father dug the ground,
I drew the lines on paper
while mother prepared the meals,
and everybody busied himself for me.

Lord,
keep my parents in your love.
Lord,
bless them and keep them.
Lord,
please let me have money and strength
and keep my parents for many more years
so that I can take care of them.   Amen.

Night over our school, prayer of a young Ghanaian Christian.

PRAYERS OF COMPASSION

" God dwells among the lowliest of men. He sits on the dust-heap among the prison convicts. With the juvenile delinquents He stands at the door, begging bread. He throngs with the beggars at the place of alms. He is among the sick. He stands in line with the unemployed in front of the free employment bureaux.

" Therefore, let him who would meet God visit the prison cell before going to the temple. Before he goes to church let him visit the hospital. Before he reads his Bible let him help the beggar standing at his door.

" If he visits the prison after going to the temple, does he not by so much delay his meeting with God ? If he goes first to the church and then to the hospital, does he not by so much postpone beholding God ? If he fails to help the beggar at his door and indulges himself in Bible-reading, there is a danger lest God, who lives among the mean, will go elsewhere. In truth he who forgets the unemployed forgets God."

Toyohiko Kagawa, Japan.

God, my Lord.
I believe that you are present everywhere.
I believe that your presence is specially found among the poor, the needy, the fatherless or motherless orphans and the sick.
By working for social justice, freedom, peace and unity, I know that I am working with you for your kingdom.
But with all this awareness I still fail to find you among the poor and the needy and hence I fail to bring about peace, unity and justice.
I still crave for power and position.
I crave for all the comforts which the world can give.
I love wealth.
I love security.
Help me, Lord, to realise the needs of those down-trodden.
Help me, Lord, to strive for the betterment of my brethren.
Help me to be a man for others.
Otherwise, give me the courage to say that I am not a Christian any more.
Amen.

Prayer of an Indian Christian.

Father, my Father, enlarge my heart that it may be big
enough to receive the greatness of thy love.   Stretch my
heart that it may take into it all those who with me around
the world believe in Jesus Christ.   Stretch it that it may
take into it all those who do not know him, but who are
my responsibility because I know him.   And stretch it that
it may take in all those who are not lovely in my eyes, and
whose hands I do not want to touch; through Jesus Christ,
my Saviour.   *The prayer of an African.*

Dearest Lord, may I see you today and every day in the
person of your sick, and, whilst nursing them, minister unto
you.

Though you hide yourself behind the unattractive disguise
of the irritable, the exacting, the unreasonable, may I still
recognise you and say: 'Jesus, my patient, how sweet it is
to serve you'.

Lord, give me this seeing faith, then my work will never be
monotonous.   I will ever find joy in humouring the fancies
and gratifying the wishes of all poor sufferers.

O beloved sick, how doubly dear you are to me, when you
personify Christ; and what a privilege is mine to be allowed
to tend you.

Sweetest Lord, make me appreciative of the dignity of my
high vocation, and its many responsibilities.   Never permit
me to disgrace it by giving way to coldness, unkindness,
or impatience.

And, O God, while you are Jesus, my patient, deign also
to be to me a patient Jesus, bearing with my faults, looking
only to my intention, which is to love and serve you in the
person of each of your sick.

Lord, increase my faith, bless my efforts and work, now and
for evermore.   Amen.
                 Daily prayer of Mother Teresa of Calcutta.

God of Infinite Mercy, bless the men and women who
languish in our prisons, our boys and girls who sit in
correction homes, and those who spend their lives in our
state hospital.   Give us to know that they are islands of
the continent of Man of which we are a part.   Amen.
                                   Prayer from Hawaii.

O Lord and heavenly Father, we commend to thy care the men, women and children of our country and of all Africa who are suffering distress and anxiety because of lack of food. Strengthen and support them, we beseech thee; and grant that the world may grow in understanding of thy ways, and in sharing all the good gifts which thou hast given us to live on in fellowship with each other, for Jesus Christ's sake.   *A prayer from Kenya for the hungry.*

Pray for us, brethren, that we may not fail in the oil of comfort, the wine of justice, the involvement of the patient mule, and the generosity which, having given, promised more, until rehabilitation was complete.

A prayer based on the parable of the
Good Samaritan, as used in Hong Kong.

Unlike men's frontiers
God's frontiers may be crossed without permit or passport.
There is a frontier I may cross
deep within my own heart.
There is a frontier I may cross
as I reach out in loving concern to another man's need.
Always I live on the frontier.

Prayer used by Congregational Prayer Fellowship.

PRAYERS FOR MUCH LOVED LANDS

For India:
We intercede before thee for beloved Hindustan
and our prayer is the same
as that of ancient seekers after thee,
'From darkness lead us to light
And from shadows to reality'.
Mercifully grant that the millions of this land
forever engaged in arduous pilgrimages
in search of peace and satisfaction
may at last lay down their weary burdens
at the feet of him who gives rest and peace
to all those who labour and are heavy laden.
May they come at last to the haven of peace,
even Jesus Christ,
and find in him thine own response
to their age-long quest.
To that end the frankincense of India's meditation,
the myrrh of its renunciation and sacrifice,
and the gold of its devotion
be laid at the feet of Jesus Christ
and may he be crowned Lord of all.

Augustine Ralla Ram.

God bless India;
Feed her hungry ones;
Heal her sorrows;
And give her Christ.

Canon Douglas Webster, written on one of
his many visits to India.

Great God of all,
bless our country!
This land which gave us birth and life
and which we love with deep devotion.

This strange and wondrous land
that is the home of such varied creeds and cultures.
Its people speaking so many different tongues,
eating, drinking, worshipping differently,
yet united in loving thee.
Dear Land,
land of mighty snow-clad mountains,
arid deserts, forests dense,
and rolling rivers,
smiling fields and barren sunbaked earth
where bounteous plenty and gaunt famine live side by side.

40

Land of light and darkness,
of colour;
of dance and music and festival,
of sadness,
    hunger,
    death and despair.
Of happiness,
    goodwill and hospitality,
of sudden passion and wanton violence.
Some rich
many not so rich.
And most of all poor.
Good people, Lord, and a good land.
But now there are danger signals.
Preserve the freedom we cherish, Lord;
grant us peace and prosperity in our time
and keep our beloved land forever in the palm of your hand.

*Day of Prayer for our country: usually observed by all
churches in India on the first Sunday in Advent.*

When shall these longings be sufficed
That stir my spirit night and day?
When shall I see my country lay
Her homage at the feet of Christ?

Yea, how behold that blissful day
When all her prophets' mystic lore
And all her ancient wisdom's store
Shall own His consummating sway?

Of all I have, O Saviour sweet,
All gifts, all skill, all thoughts of mine,
A living garland I entwine,
And offer at Thy lotus feet.

Narayan Vaman Tilak: Christian poet of Maharashtra.

For Nepal:

O Lord, hear our petition, open the door of salvation
For the Gorkhalis.
Father, Son, Holy Spirit, hear our petition,
Show us the way by a cloudy fiery pillar.
Peoples of different religions are to east, west, and south;
Tibet is north, and Nepal our home in the middle.
There are cities; Thapathali, Bhatgaon, Patan, Kathmandu:
Our desire is to make them your devotees.
Up, brothers: we must go, ignoring hate and shame,
Leaving wealth, people, comfort, to do the holy task.

*Prayer-hymn of Nepali Christians, prayed
over many years on the borders of Nepal.*

For Pakistan:
God guide Pakistan
at work and at prayer
at home and abroad
and, by wise teachers
and good leaders,
bring her many people to the gate
of that kingdom where
the sudden sight of your beauty
will dull all pain
wipe away all tears
heal all wounds
quicken all consciences
and draw from all men the response:
through Jesus Christ our Lord!

Amen.

O Lord, be gracious unto our land of Pakistan,
give strength to its poor,
compassion to its rich,
wisdom to its leaders,
and, to its common people,
the will to make it truly pure.

Amen.

For Iran:
God protect this country from foe, famine, and falsehood.

2,000 year old Irani prayer.

Now may the Spirit, who gave the Word, and called me, I
trust, to be an interpreter of it, graciously and powerfully
apply it to the hearts of sinners, even to the gathering of an
elect people from amongst the long-estranged Persians.

*Prayer of Henry Martyn, as recorded in his diary on
February 24, 1812, the day he finished the
translation of the New Testament into Persian.*

For Israel:
O God of Abraham, Isaac, and Jacob, grant that
Israel of today may inherit the callings and
blessings of Israel of old.
May it be
a God-ruled nation within itself
a nation of priests to the world
a blessing to all nations
a joy to the whole earth.
Revive, O Lord God
the gift of prophecy
the perception of your will

the speaking of your Word.
Deepen, O Lord,
a sense of responsibility for the world
the care for the stranger, the homeless and the poor
the consciousness of your judgement.
Let it look afresh
to its son Jesus of Nazareth
to the Church which developed from itself
to all its Semitic brethren
to the House of Islam sharing in some degree its faith in you.
So that it may accomplish
your purpose for the world and for itself.
O Holy One of Israel,
O God of all.   *George Appleton, Jerusalem Prayers.*

O Eternal Lord God, in time past Thou didst speak through
a flame of fire in the Sinai desert, and so didst set in motion
the promulgation of Thy Law.   Thou art speaking again—
through another flame—warning men of tragedies that
inevitably follow if they will not keep Thy Law and work it
out in human society.   Let this tragic death-dealing flame
be a sign to the nations, and a guide line to righteousness
and peace, O Creator God, Sovereign Lord, Righteous
Judge and Merciful Redeemer.

Prayer used at Memorial Service in Jerusalem,
and attended by Jews and Christians and a handful
of Muslims, following the shooting down of the
Libyan plane in the Sinai desert, 1973.

For the Middle East:
God bless the countries of the Middle East
Guard their children
Guide their leaders
Grant them peace with justice
for Jesus Christ's sake.

O Lord, we beseech thee, grant thy blessing and guidance
to all who are seeking to bring peace to the Middle East;
stir the conscience of the nations, and break the bonds of
covetousness; make plain thy way of deliverance: through
Jesus Christ our Lord.   Amen.

A prayer used in the Diocese of Hong Kong and Macao:
Grant, dear Lord, to all the people in Hong Kong,
in trouble, peace;
in hardship, joy;
and at all times a quiet mind, trusting in thee.

For Sabah:

From all dangers, and temptations too strong,
Good Lord, deliver us.
From floods that sweep away homes, livestock and produce,
Good Lord, deliver us.
From storms which blow off roof-tops,
Good Lord, deliver us.
From falling through floors, off bamboo bridges, or out of boats.
Good Lord, deliver us.
From lack of boats, boatmen, petrol and engines,
Good Lord, deliver us.
From storms at sea, and rapids in the river,
Good Lord, deliver us.
From too fast launches, which overturn or swamp our boats,
Good Lord, deliver us.
From breakdowns in radio communications,
Good Lord, deliver us.
From lack of medical and educational supplies,
Good Lord, deliver us.
From material hardships caused by lack of financial support,
Good Lord, deliver us.
From Malaria, T.B. and dysentry,
Good Lord, deliver us.
From snakes, scorpions, centipedes, and all harmful creatures,
Good Lord, deliver us.
From mosquitoes, boring beatles, ants and caterpillars,
Good Lord, deliver us.
O Lord, for those who seek to serve you in Tongud we pray;
Keep them in the knowledge of your abiding presence,
O hear us, Good Lord.
Help them to keep a sense of proportion, and a sense of
humour,
O hear us, Good Lord.
Give them your gifts of patience and understanding always,
O hear us, Good Lord.
Save them from misunderstandings so easily caused by
linguistic and cultural differences,
O hear us, Good Lord.
Help them to keep a firm hold on what they know to be
true,
O hear us, Good Lord.
We pray that vocations to the Sacred Ministry may be found
among the people of Sabah,
O hear us, Good Lord.
We pray that sufficient teachers may be found to staff all
Christian schools,
O hear us, Good Lord.
Forgive us, O Lord, that we are too often fearful and
doubting,
Lord Jesus, have mercy.
Forgive us when we put our own comfort and safety before
that of our fellows,
Lord Jesus, have mercy.

Forgive us that we take the people's generosity and kindness
to us for granted,
Lord Jesus, have mercy.
Forgive us that we are so often superior and condescending
in our attitude,
Lord Jesus, have mercy.
Forgive us our lack of love,
Lord Jesus, have mercy.

O Lord God, may we show forth your praise not only with
our lips, but in our lives; by giving up ourselves to your
service, and in the service of those for whom our Lord Jesus
Christ died. May your people find freedom from fear; may
they receive healing of soul, mind and body. This we ask
for the sake of Jesus Christ, our Lord. Amen.

A Tongud Litany from Sabah.

For Japan:

We beseech thee, O God Almighty, that thou grant us the
power to do thy will and to be of service to thy holy
purpose, preparing the way to build up the kingdom here in
the Orient.
Let us learn to do everything for the ministry of reconcilia-
tion and redemption, to heal the wounded souls and to
restore the broken hearts, that we may strengthen the ties of
the Christian fellowship between the nations of the world.
We lift our hearts to thee, O God our Lord, in the genuine
desire to share each other's burdens with our fellow
Christians of every nation. In the name of our Saviour,
Jesus Christ, our Lord.

Akira Ebisawa.

Take Thou the burden, Lord;
I am exhausted with this heavy load,
My tired hands tremble,
And I stumble, stumble
Along the way.
Oh, lead with Thine unfailing arm
Again today.

Unless Thou lead me, Lord,
The road I journey on is all too hard.
Through trust in Thee alone
Can I go on.

Yet not for self alone
Thus do I groan;
My people's sorrows are the load I bear.
Lord, hear my prayer—
May Thy strong hand
Strike off all chains
That load my well-loved land.
God, draw her close to Thee.

Toyohiko Kagawa.

For China:

We praise thee, our Father, that even in the hour of darkness
we can come to thee with confidence and unflinching
faith.

We know that thou art the ruler of nations and the maker
of history; we know that nothing that men can do can ever
frustrate thy holy and righteous will; we know that thou
canst make even the wrath of men to praise thee.

Help us, Father, to learn the lessons that have come out of
conflict; help us to work for the new day that will bring us
one step nearer thy kingdom.

Dear Lord and Father of mankind, grant that the day may
not be too far off when the nations will become one, when
war will be abolished, and when we shall all live peacefully
together as brethren in thy holy family.

A Chinese Christian.

Almighty God, who has built thy Church upon the
foundations of the Apostles and Prophets, and has declared
by thy Blessed Son that the gates of Hell shall not prevail
against it: guide, guard and prosper, we pray thee, the
Chung Hua Sheng Kung Hui, that abiding ever under thy
protection and seeking ever to fulfil thy will, it may turn
many to righteousness, and may be the means of advancing
unity, peace and godliness among all Christian people in
China, to the praise of thy Holy Name; through Jesus
Christ our Lord.

Bishop Charles Perry Scott's prayer for
the Chung Hua Sheng Kung Hui,
the Chinese Holy Catholic Church.

For Africa:

God bless Africa:
Guard her children,
Guide her rulers,
And give her peace.
For Jesus Christ's sake.

Bishop Huddleston's prayer for Africa.

Tanganyika, bless the Lord
And all your tribes and districts
Bless the Lord
Praise and extol Him for ever and ever.

All you *big* things, bless the Lord
Mount Kilimanjaro and Lake Victoria
The Rift Valley and the Serengeti Plain
Fat baobabs and shady mango trees
All eucalyptus and tamarind trees
Bless the Lord
Praise and extol Him for ever and ever.

All you *tiny* things, bless the Lord
Busy black ants and hopping fleas
Wriggling tadpoles and mosquito larvae
Flying locusts and water drops
Pollen dust and tsetse flies
Millet seeds and dried dagaa
Bless the Lord
Praise and extol Him for ever and ever.

All you *sharp* things, bless the Lord
Sisal plant tips and tall lake reeds
Masai spears and hunting arrows
A rhino's horn and the crocodile teeth
Bless the Lord
Praise and extol him for ever and ever.

All you *soft* things, bless the Lord
Sawdust and ashes and kapok wool
Sponges and porridge and golden-ripe mangoes
Bless the Lord
Praise and extol him for ever and ever.

All you *sweet* things, bless the Lord
Wild honey and pawpaws and coconut milk
Pineapple and sugar cane and sun-dried dates
Slow-roasted yams and banana juice
Bless the Lord
Praise and extol him for ever and ever.

All you *bitter* things, bless the Lord
Quinine and blue soap
Sour milk and maize beer
Bless ye the Lord
Praise and extol Him for ever and ever.

All you *swift* things, bless the Lord
Wild goats and honking lorries
Frightened centipedes and lightning flashes
Bless ye the Lord
Praise and extol him for ever and ever.

All you *slow* things, bless ye the Lord
Curious giraffes and old bony cows
Long-tailed chameleons, grass-munching sheep
Bless ye the Lord
Praise and extol him for ever and ever.

All you *loud* things, bless the Lord
Monsoon rains on aluminium roofs
Midnight hyenas and feast-day drums
Train stations and carpenters shops
Bless the Lord
Praise and extol him for ever and ever.

All you *quiet* things, bless the Lord
Candle flames and just-sown furrows
Heaps of clouds and sunny libraries
Our Uluguru Mountains and sleeping pupas
Land snails and crawling turtles
Grazing zebras and stalking lions
Bless the Lord
Praise and extol Him for ever and ever.

All you creatures that never talk
Still, bless ye the Lord
Praise and extol Him for ever and ever.

An African Canticle.

Grant us, O God, a vision of our land, fair as she might be: a
land of justice, where none shall prey on others; a land of
plenty, where poverty shall cease to fester; a land of
brotherhood, where success shall be founded on service;
a land of peace, where order shall not rest on force, but
on the love of all for their country, and give us grace to put
this vision into practice, through Jesus Christ our Lord.

A prayer commended by the Christian
Council of Nigeria.

PRAYERS FOR FREEDOM

A certain man went through a forest seeking any bird of interest he might find. He caught a young eagle, brought it home and put it among his fowls and ducks and turkeys, and gave it chicken's food to eat even though it was an eagle, the king of birds.

Five years later a naturalist came to see him and, after passing through his garden, said: 'That bird is an eagle, not a chicken.'

' Yes,' said its owner, ' but I have trained it to be a chicken. It is no longer an eagle, it is a chicken, even though it measures fifteen feet from tip to tip of its wings.'

' No, ' said the naturalist, ' it is an eagle still: it has the heart of an eagle, and I will make it soar high up to the heavens.'

'No,' said the owner,' it is a chicken, and it will never fly.'

They agreed to test it. The naturalist picked up the eagle, held it up, and said with great intensity: 'Eagle, thou art an eagle; thou dost belong to the sky and not to this earth; stretch forth thy wings and fly.'

The eagle turned this way and that, and then, looking down, saw the chickens eating their food, and down he jumped.

Then the owner said: 'I told you it was a chicken.'

' No ', asserted the naturalist, 'it is an eagle, and it still has the heart of an eagle; only give it one more chance, and I will make it fly tomorrow.'

The next morning he rose early and took the eagle outside the city, away from the houses, to the foot of a high mountain. The sun was just rising, gilding the top of the mountain with gold, and every crag was glistening in the joy of that beautiful morning.

He picked up the eagle and said to it: 'Eagle, thou art an eagle; thou dost belong to the sky and not to this earth; stretch forth thy wings and fly!'

The eagle looked round and trembled as if new life were coming to it; but it did not fly. The naturalist then made it look straight at the sun. Suddenly it stretched out its wings and, with the screech of an eagle, it mounted higher and higher and never returned. It was an eagle, though it had been kept and tamed as a chicken!

My people of Africa, we were created in the image of God, but men have made us think that we are chickens, and we still think we are; but we are eagles.   Stretch forth your wings and fly!   Don't be content with the food of chickens!

The Parable of the Eagle—James Aggrey.

As we were walking I noticed many young children of school age curiously looking at me.   There were, apparently no schools for them.   I said 'hello' to them a few times, but there was no response.   My guide whispered to me: 'Say "freedom" and see what happens.'   So I shouted to the children" freedom ", and instantly all the children like one mighty army shouted back, now with a big smile on their faces.

Daisuke Kitagawa, one time staff member of the Department of Church and Society, WCC, on a visit to Zambia.

O Thou, who art the Lion of Judah,
    be thou also the Lion of Africa,
    and burst all the chains
that still bind our African brothers,
and deliver them from all fear.   Amen.

O Lord, help us who roam about.   Help us who have been placed in Africa and have no dwelling place of our own. Give us back our dwelling place.

Prayer used in 1947 by the late chief of the Hereros, Hosea Kutako, in entrusting Michael Scott with the mission of persuading the UN to take up Namibia's case.

Almighty God, who hast known sorrow when thy people were slaves in Egypt and captives in Babylon, and who knowest sorrow now in Africa and Mississippi, forgive us when we do not know what we do—and even when we do. Amen.   *Prayer from Hawaii.*

O God, who hast made the earth so varied and cast the races of men in so many different moulds, we who dwell in these lovely islands of the western sea pray for all thy children.   Grant that through the power of Jesus Christ we may be freed from such spiritual shackles as still enslave us, that in his light all darkness of superstition may be dispelled, and that we may enter into the full joyous life of thy kingdom.   *Prayer of a West Indian Christian.*

Women:	Where children walk without fear, heads held high;
Men:	Where knowledge for all youth is free;
Women:	Where society has not been broken into fragments by narrow domestic walls;
Men:	Where the words of teachers and politicians spring out from the depths of truth;
Women:	Where the tireless striving of social reformers stretches its arms towards perfection;
Men:	Where the clear stream of creative culture has not lost its way into the desert sand of dead habit;
Women:	Where the minds of leaders, scientists and writers are led forward by thee into ever-widening thought and action;

Into that divinely given freedom, Father of all, let our country awake.

*Adapted from Rabindranath Tagore's prayer
for true freedom; Worship for Independence
Day, Andhra Christian Theological College,
Hyderabad.*

I see
centuries of oppression,
deceit, viciousness,
on your sick face.

You see
centuries of submission,
credibility, servility,
on my black face.

Persist
in your delusion,
I will not
disturb your illusion.

Yet.

D. Appadurai, India.

The other day, I smacked the air, you know.
It hit me hard; it hurt my hand.
    " Air is not for me."
    " Then why not earth ?"
    " Yes! I'll build with earth—
Build what I like and where."

But earth did fly from me to heaven.
It wished to settle there.
    " To hell with it, " I said.
    " Water still is mine. "
I rinsed my eyes; they felt so cool.
I squeezed them, then I drank.
My eyes are not fast coloured, so they ran.
My water turned to black, and
In my mouth
It froze—
Like darkness
Frozen
In a cave
    " Fire! " was now my cry.
    " I'll burn my toe.
    I love the pain, the ashes and the flame. "

My toe, it burned.
But more than that—
    the fire leapt
    and caught the rest.

Yasmin Abassi, Pakistan.
Life is all against the Pakistani girl. Rather
petulantly she takes it out on the elements—
air, earth, water, and finally fire.

O God, please make me a boy in my next life.
Prayer of a Hindu village girl, Orissa.

52

PRAYERS OF FOLLOWING

Lead us not into imitation.

Prayer of East Asia Christian Council Youth
Consultation, in a report which bears on its
cover a coca-cola bottle, superimposed on a
map of Asia.

O God, we pray to thee amid the perplexities of a changing order. Help us to learn new ways that thou wouldest teach us, and in every unknown path give us boldness to follow him who is the same Saviour yesterday, today and forever.

Adapted from prayer used in Mengo
Hospital, Uganda.

O God, I am Mustafah the tailor and I work at the shop of Muhammad Ali. The whole day long I sit and pull the needle and the thread through the cloth. O God, you are the needle, and I am the thread. I am attached to you and I follow you. When the thread tries to slip away from the needle it becomes tangled up and must be cut so that it can be put back in the right place. O God, help me to follow you wherever you may lead me. For I am really only Mustafah, the tailor, and I work at the shop of Muhammad Ali on the great square.

A Muslim who had just come to follow Christ
said his first prayer as a Christian in these
words.

O God, Thou knowest that I do not want anything else but to serve Thee and men, always, all my life. Amen.

Temple Gairdner of Cairo, first audible prayer.

Merciful, O merciful
Mother Mary's
Great Son,
Give to me bread of peace.
When crossing distant paths
I have heard your name
From your fervent followers
From John and from Luke
From dedicated clergy
Serving in the church
On all their lips
You are the treasury of peace.

Overwhelmed with the venomous poison of this world
Trapped by this world of illusion
This follower waits, O merciful
For your call.
Turn your merciful look to me
Then you will see my sorrows.
I have come to you
I am wearied
Of treading the paths of this world.
I am burdened
With the burden of this earth,
Lord, now draw me back to you.

Firoz Uddin, a Bengali Muslim follower of Jesus.

Lord, I want to be lazy. For some days I want to escape from this active world to a region of laziness where I can wander about watching stray children playing about, enjoying the communal life of the birds, sitting and gazing at the tireless tides.

I want to climb that hill where the world lies far behind and the heavens seem still more far.

In that garden I want to move about playing with doves, plucking flowers and eating mango fruits.

I want to sit still upon my easy chair looking at the mirror and talking to myself.

I want to have a nap and sometimes a sleep. Then I want to bathe in the river and flow with the water. I like playing upon the river bank and hiding in the sugar cane grove— Lord, I want to be lazy.

I Want to be Lazy—meditations of an Indian
Christian.

Lord, show us deeply how important it is to be useless.

Bangkok prayer.

In order to live a fully rounded life, life as God intends it to be, we must include things other than our work. This almost inevitably means leaving something undone. For us, planned neglect will mean deliberately choosing which things we will leave undone or postpone, so that instead of being oppressed by a clutter of unfinished jobs, we think out our priorities under God and then accept without guilt or resentment the fact that much that we had thought we ought to do we must leave.

We shall often be tempted into guilty feelings when we do take time off. But we should then remind ourselves that such guilt is a sin against the generosity of the Spirit, and also extremely infectious.

Planned neglect—The Companions of
Brother Lawrence: Rule of Life.

The Spinning Top:
Lord, we are so top-heavy; our whole structure—
In Session, Synod, Council, and Assembly—
The whole thing topples, and to keep from falling,
We, top-like, spin and spin on our own axis,
Self-centred, humming, whipped to static fury;
And so gyrating, pride ourselves on action.

Lord, knock us sideways, send us spinning outwards;
Uncentre us from self, and make our axis
That transverse axle-tree, the Cross, that turning
On Christ alone we may roll forward, steady,
To that great day, when, every creature gospelled,
The end shall come, and nations see the Glory.

Robin Boyd, Gujarat, North India.

Lord,
so eager was I for Thy darshan
that I donned the yellow robes of a sannyasi.
I walked the dusty, weary miles
of the road from Dravida to the Himalayas
in my bare feet.

I endured the heat of noonday,
the lash of monsoon tempests,
the perils of tortuous jungle paths.
Lonely forest shrines echoed to my kirtans
when I offered juna with garlands of wild flowers.
But nowhere did I find Thee . . .

And then suddenly I met Thee,
met Thee walking the roads
of my own heart.   *Darshan: prayer of an Indian Christian.*

PRAYER FOR MISSIONARIES

Pack up your baggage quick and get you gone,
All whom the land of India pleaseth not.
Think not that money or authority
Can save us; ' tis a false and vain conceit.
Fathers and godlings we desire not these;
Come, let us knit the bonds of brotherhood
Say servant Tilak, Be the time that's past forgot,
And a new mind put on in this new day.

Narayan Vaman Tilak, Christian poet of Maharashtra.

If you cannot understand what is happening in this
continent, in this hour in which it awakens to the dawn of
a new liberation: *Missionary go home.*

If you are not able to separate the eternal world of the
Gospel from the cultural moulds in which you brought it to
these lands and even taught it with true abnegation:
Missionary go home.

If you cannot identify with the sufferings, anguish and
aspirations of these peoples made prematurely old by an
unequal struggle that would seem not to have end or hope:
Missionary go home.

If your allegiance and fidelity to the nation of your origin is
stronger than your loyalty and obedience to Jesus Christ,
who has come ' to put down the mighty from their thrones
and exalt those of low degree ': *Missionary go home.*

If your dogmatism is such that it does not permit you to
revise your theology and ideology in the light of all the
Biblical testimony and the happenings of these times:
Missionary go home.

If you are not able to love and respect as equals those whom
one day you came to evangelise as lost: *Missionary go
home.*

If you cannot rejoice with the entrance of new peoples and
churches into a new maturity, of independence, of responsibility, even at the price of committing errors such as those
you and your countrymen committed also in the past:
Then it is time to return home.

But, if you are willing to share the risks and pains of this hour of birth in which our peoples are living, even denying yourself; if you begin to rejoice with them because of the joy of feeling that the Gospel is not only the announcement and affirmation of a remote hope, but of a hope and a liberation that is already transforming history; if you are willing to put more of your time, of your values, of your life at the service of these people who are awakening; *then stay.* For there is much to be done, and hands and blood are needed for such an immense enterprise in which Christ is pioneer and protagonist.

Missionary Litany; Fedrico Pagura, Methodist Bishop of Costa Rica.

Dear Lord,
our pastor and teacher, brother Lewis
is leaving us.
As we say here: " for good."

Lord,
we are sad, but we know
that it is You who are calling him back.

Lord,
he was ten years with us.

Lord,
You blessed us through him,
we thank You for this man, our brother,
teacher and preacher, but he was more—
Your humble servant
and our brother in the flesh.

Lord,
he gave us the best years of his life.
Despite his titles from Oxford,
he sat with us in the bush and
came to our houses,
learned Twi
and preached in our language.
He was always simple
and he soon lost his heavy accent.

Lord,
he did not stay only in our village;
he went to the huts of the Ewes
who are living in the mountains,
who cultivate their poor soil
and who live in fear of their idols.

He learned Ewe
and many heard him witnessing:
" Be not afraid—
the great God over all idols is with you. "

Lord,
the distinguished school of Achimota
wanted him;
the University
offered him a professorship,
but he stayed with us,
Lord,
how You did bless us through this man.

Lord,
he lived in Your grace
and shouted in English, Twi and Ewe:
" Proclaim the Lord! "

Lord,
we, his brothers and sisters,
the Twis and Ewes,
ask your blessing for him:
Bless his family, his wife and children.

Lord,
comfort them in their sadness
when they leave Africa.
Bring them safely to the port of Liverpool,
Let them begin their new service
with gladness.
Lord,
bless them,
our prayers go with them.
Lord,
when they rejoice,
we will add our hallelujah;
Lord,
when they mourn, we shall cry.

Lord,
Be with Your faithful servants.
We all pray for this.
Amen.

Brother Lewis is leaving us: Prayer of young
Ghanaian Christians.

O Lord,
you know that we are still hungry
so bring them back to teach us.

Prayer of a Sudanese pastor for the return
of missionaries.

O Lord of the Vineyard, we thank thee that the seed of the Vine planted in the many countries of Asia has taken root and grown.   Continue we beseech thee to send labourers into the vineyard.   Strengthen the Churches of Asia against all temptations.   Grant that they may bear much fruit and thus glorify thy name. Amen.

In Malayalam, prayer offered by Indian delegate at World Missionary Conference, Edinburgh, 1910.

THE THIRD WORLD CLAIMS
A SHARE IN COMMEMORATING
THE LIFE OF OUR LORD

Advent:

Art Thou a stranger to my country, Lord?
My land of black roots and thick jungles
where the wild boar sharpens his tusks,
where the monkeys chatter in the trees,
and the peacock's shrill note
echoes through the mist-clad hills;
my land of brown, caked river mud
where the elephant and the leopard come to drink,
and the shambling bear with his dreamy eyes
sees the porcupine shedding his quills;
my land with its friezes of palmyra palms
etched sharply against the blue mountains;
my land of low-lying plains
with its miles of murmuring paddy fields
that stretch in undulating waves of green
to the distant horizon;
my land of sapphire skies and flaming sunsets,
my land of leaden grey skies piled high
with banks of monsoon clouds;
my land of stinging rain, of burning heat,
of dark nights, of enchanting moons
that dance behind the coconut fronds;
my land of tanks and pools
where the lazy buffalo wallows
and the red lotuses lie asleep?
Nay, Thou art no stranger, Lord,
for the wind whispers of Thee
and the waters chant Thy name.
The whole land is hushed in trembling expectancy,
awaiting Thy touch of creative Love.

Advent: Chandran Devanesen, India.

The Nativity:
Dear Master,
May Thy Light
Shine on me now,
As once it shone
Upon the Shepherds,
As they kept their flocks
By night.

Prayer of Ozaki, a Japanese leprosy patient.

O God, who before all other didst call shepherds to the cradle of thy Son: Grant that by the preaching of the gospel the poor, the humble, and the forgotten, may know that they are at home with thee; through Jesus Christ our Lord. Amen.

The Book of Common Worship,
Church of South India.

Hush Thee, hush Thee, baby Christ,
  Lord of all mankind;
Thou the happy lullaby
  Of my mind.

Hush Thee, hush Thee, Jesus, Lord,
  Stay of all Thou art;
Thou the happy lullaby
  Of my heart.

Hush Thee, hush Thee, Home of peace—
  Lo, Love lying there;
Thou the happy lullaby
  Of my care.

Hush Thee, hush Thee, Soul of mine,
  Setting all men free;
Thou the happy lullaby
  Of the whole of me.

Narayan Vaman Tilak: Marathi Christian poet.

Let not our souls be busy inns that have no room for Thee and Thine, but quiet homes of prayer and praise where Thou mayest find fit company; where the needful cares of life are wisely ordered and put away; and wide sweet spaces kept for Thee, where holy thoughts pass up and down, and fervent longings watch and wait Thy coming.

Prayer suggested for use in the Lucknow
Diocese, North India.

Budoshu wo
  Isasaka sugoshi
  Seiya kana.

And there are also those
  Who just a whit do over-celebrate
  Their Christmas Eve.

Haiku: Tetsuzo Takeda, Japan.

The Holy Innocents:
I meet him every moment
Your Son and our Brother Christ,
Hunger causes physical, mental and moral damage.
When I see the children of my people,
the Silent World,
wasted away, stomach distended,
heads enormous and often very empty,
retarded as if it were missing,
it is Christ that I see.

Mother, we understand each other so well
that I have no need to explain
or ask you anything.
I shall keep your statue
with the deformed Child
as in life, as in our world,
in which egoism breeds monsters.
Even when the Third World
gains a head and a voice,
the Child will continue to be headless
as a remembrance of the days of sorrow
that will belong for ever in the past.

> *Archbishop Helder Camara of Brazil.*
> *The verses are about a stone statue of the*
> *Blessed Virgin Mary holding the Child.*
> *The Child's head had been broken off.*
> *People had suggested that a new head*
> *should be carved. ' No ', was the answer.*
> *And so the Archbishop addresses the Virgin*
> *Mary in the words of this prayer.*

He shall be round our necks till the end of time.
We have loved him, and have desired something splendid,
Imagined something great and good. We have hoped
Each temper and trial will be ours to harvest;
Thought, of each public shame and private rejection,
This is the hardest we shall ever bear;
Time will be when the steepest climb is ended;
This is the last voyage; we shall come at last to harbour.
But perhaps, father, it is time to understand
There will be no answer. There will be no end of hoping,
And the arms that hate you even when they cling
Shall be round your neck for ever. Time, mother,
To know you are a mother indeed, and had better
Like Mary, find the joy of it here and now.

> *Abnormal Child, prayer/poem of missionary in Japan.*

Flight into Egypt:

We will receive you Lord
For want of a better name
If you can have us as we are
Black skinned, inclined to love
Our human kind.

We will receive you with drums
Dancing and prodigal feasting
Not as an intermediary
To God or truth
On special days and Sundays.

We do not befriend
Mortal or spiritual dictators
But comprehend the glory of your message
So wasted; which rings however dimly in our ears.
Thought before action; others before self
So never letting the confounded world go by
Without adieu.

Gambian poet and novelist Lenrie Peters.

God of grace and providence, Lord of our going out and of
our coming in, we pray for Egypt, shelter of the Holy
Family from the old tyranny of Herod and first resting
place beyond the manger of the eternal glory.   Bless her
land and people, once entertaining unawares the earth's
redeemer.   Make the Church in Egypt the patient means
to Thy purpose and ready custodian of the peace of Christ,
ever left with His servants and ever passing through and
from them for the saving of the world.   We pray in His
Name.   Amen.

Bishop Kenneth Cragg.

Epiphany:

O Lord almighty who has mysteriously revealed to the sages
of old your ineffable presence in the depth of the heart,
grant to us and also to those of our brothers who follow
in their footsteps that being led by your holy Spirit in this
inward search we may discover therein the light incor-
ruptible, your divine Son, Jesus Christ our Lord, ever and
ever. Amen.

The Holy Eucharist: Forms of Worship,
Jyotiniketan Ashram, North India and
Jerusalem.

O small Lord of the whole world
to whom at your Epiphany
came men, discerning,
offering gifts, gold, frankincense and myrrh;
India's gift came late, prevented,
rain-washed, flood-drenched,
sun-baked, dust-covered,
yet still on time.

If not for birth, at least for death;
spikenard by Mary of Magdala's hand,
reared and compounded on Himalayan hills,
and Joseph's gift—who also gave a tomb—
a winding sheet from hottest Sind
for that cool body.

Of birth (they say) this land knows more
than most
of death, still more.
Its constant gathering place
the burial plot, as young
and old in Indian years
are laid to rest.

With Mary's outpoured balm
and Joseph's finest cloth
sent by this land,
accept the gift of this folk's fortitude,
and laying hold on these her gifts
touch also the giver and her monstrous dying
with the hope of the world's resurrection.   Amen.

Prayer for Pakistan.

Two thousand years have slipped by
like freshets in the Ganges
since St. Thomas came to our land.
Here, though the cross is lifted
amidst the paddy fields and coconut palms
and white-clad Christians flock to the churches
when the bells call them to worship;
our wise men have not yet seen the star
and the manger of Bethlehem
is not yet the cradle of our land.
But Christian hope never dies
and the ends of the strands of destiny
are held safe in the hands of God.

Pass it on to the ends of the earth!
Christ is the answer—Ours!   Yours!

Chandran Devanesen, India.

64

O merciful God, who, when thou didst send thy son into
the world, didst grant to certain Magi from the East the
honour of admittance to the presence of that Blessed Babe;
grant that we, the Persians of this century may enter into
the holy inheritance of our forefathers, and bow before him,
who with thee and the Holy Ghost, liveth and reigneth one
God for ever.   Amen.

Additional Collect for the Epiphany, Iran.

O God, who by a star didst guide the Wise Men to the
worship of thy Son: lead, we pray thee, to thyself the wise
and the great in every land, that unto thee every knee may
bow, and every thought be brought into captivity; through
Jesus Christ our Lord.

The Book of Common Worship: Church of South India.

Minister:	From delusion to truth, and into your righteous way:
People:	Lead us, Father God.
Minister:	From darkness to light, and into your gracious will:
People:	Lead us, saviour Christ.
Minister:	From death to immortality, and into your joyful presence:
People:	Lead us, Powerful Spirit.
Minister:	Triune God, Saviour and strength of us all:
People:	It is you we worship and adore.

Ancient Bridhadaranyaka prayer, adapted for
use in worship at Andhra Christian
Theological College, Hyderabad.

One Holy Person of the Trinity, the Christ of God,
        the light of heaven and earth,
As man appeared among the sons of men: concealed His
        glorious majesty and worth,
The angels in the world above rejoiced: the vault of
        heaven rang with joy and mirth.
To shepherds watching in the fields at night they
        brought the tidings of His holy birth.

From a pure virgin by Divine command appeared the
    light that lighteneth man's days.
A brilliant star proclaimed the glad event: in the
    far heaven shone its ardent blaze.
The Persian Magi saw the effulgent star, illumining
    the sky like solar rays.
Towards Bethlehem with joyful steps they sped to
    offer him their precious gifts and praise.

Translation of Persian verse by a modern
Shiraz poet, Hamidi, in Church of Saint
Simon the Zealot, Shiraz, Iran.

The Holy Childhood:

Lord, who was born in poverty in the village of Bethlehem,
look in mercy on the people of our villages.

Thou, who growing to manhood in the village of Nazareth,
didst honour the work of men's hands by thy toil in the
carpenter's shop, look in mercy upon our village labourers
and craftsmen.

Thou who didst have a tender care for the village people,
going about amongst them, feeding the hungry, healing the
sick, and bringing light to the darkened in mind, have pity
upon all sufferers in the villages.   Friend of publicans and
sinners, have mercy on those amongst us who have gone
astray into evil paths.

Thou who didst come to preach the gospel to the poor, and
proclaim deliverance to the captives and sight to the blind,
drive our from our people the spirit of fear and let thy
light shine forth upon them, O Thou Son of Righteousness.

Prayer used in daily worship at the
Christukula Ashram in Tirappatur, South India.

My prayer-bird was cold—would not away,
Although I set it on the edge of the nest.
Then I bethought me of the story old—
Love-fact or loving fable, thou knowest best—
How, when the children had made sparrows of clay,
Thou mad'st them birds, with wings to flutter and fold:
Take, Lord, my prayer in thy hand and make it pray.

Based on story of the child Jesus in the
Apocryphal Gospel of Thomas: source unknown.

The Ministry:

O loving Father, make me like Jesus:
The Jesus who could spend nights in prayer,
The Jesus who went about doing good,
The Jesus who made time to talk to Nicodemus,
The Jesus who could not bear to see the mother cry at Nain,
The Jesus who took a towel and knelt and washed the feet
of the men who were going to deny, betray and forsake him,
The Jesus who could give a patient word when smitten on
the face,
The Jesus who could pray for the men who nailed him to
the Cross,
The Jesus who was strong enough not to answer back
when accused unjustly,
The Jesus who could sleep peacefully in a gale and storm,
The Jesus who would not let the marriage at Cana be spoilt
by lack of wine,
The Jesus who would not condemn the woman taken in an
act of sin,
The Jesus who could shrink from the cup of suffering yet
drink it to the last dregs.
O Loving Father, make me like the Jesus who came to the
world to show what you were like.

*Personal prayer of Bishop Jacob, Bishop of
Travancore, South India.*

A Litany of the Disciples of the Servant.

Servant—Christ, help us to follow you
deep into the waters of Baptism,
to link our lives with all those grieved
about man's unjust way of life;
to break free from the chain of past wrongs;
to become fit to face your coming new age;
to be renewed by your Spirit, anointed to preach good news
to the poor, the oppressed and the prisoner:

Help us to follow you, Christ the servant

Help us to follow you far into the desert, with you to fast,
denying false luxury, refusing the tempting ways
of personal satisfaction, and unscrupulous persuasion:

Help us to follow you, Christ the servant

Help us to follow you in untiring ministry to town and village,
to heal and restore the broken body of humanity,
to cast out the demonic forces of greed, resentment,
communal hatred, and self-destructive fear:

Help us to follow you, Christ the servant

Help us to follow you in to the place of quiet retreat,
to intercede for the confused, the despairing,
the anxiety-driven,
to prepare ourselves for costly service with you:

Help us to follow you, Christ the servant

Help us to follow you on the road to Jerusalem,
to set our faces firmly against friendly suggestions for a safe,
expedient life, to embrace boldly the way of self-offering, of
life given for others' gain:

Help us to follow you, Christ the servant

Help us to follow you into the city,
to claim its whole life for God whose image man bears,
to confront the ambitions of the power-hungry,
the inhuman orthodoxy of the legalist, with the startling
message of your present action, your living power:

Help us to follow you Christ the servant

Help us to follow you into the temple of your chosen
people, to erase from the worship of your Church all that
hinders the sense of your presence, the free flow of your
Word; to open up your house so that it may be a house of
prayer for all people:

Help us to follow you, Christ the servant

Help us to follow you into the upper room,
to share your meal of bread and cup,
to accept our common place in your one Body,
broken to create a New Man:

Help us to follow you, Christ the servant

Help us to follow you into the garden,
to watch with you, ever vigilant for signs
of the dawning of your new day, to struggle unsparingly
to understand and to carry out your perfect will:

Help us to follow you, Christ the servant

Help us to follow you into the judgement hall,
to stand mocked and condemned
for daring to speak direct of divine forgiveness,
daring to claim God's personal commissioning,
daring to disrupt the plans of unscrupulous leaders
for the control of the masses;
to stand for those whose right to stand has been usurped:

Help us to follow you, Christ the servant

Help us to follow you even unto the Cross,
to share in carrying your cross like Simon the African,
to recognise our life in your death,
our hope in your self-spending love,
to die to all within us that is not born of your love :

Help us to follow you, Christ the servant

Help us to follow you out of the dark tomb,
to share daily your resurrection life,
to be renewed daily in your image of love,
to be used daily as your new Body
in your service to the world:

Help us to follow you, Christ the servant.
                                    Amen.
               A Litany of the Disciples of the Servant used
               in Andhra Theological College, Hyderabad.

Father,
who hast made all men in thy likeness
and lovest all whom thou hast made,
suffer not our family to separate itself from thee
by building barriers of race and colour.

As thy Son our Saviour was born of a Hebrew mother, but
rejoiced in the faith of a Syrian woman and of a Roman
soldier, welcomed the Greeks who sought him,
and suffered a man from Africa to carry his Cross,
so teach us to regard the members of all races as fellow-
heirs of the kingdom of Jesus Christ our Lord.
                              Prayer used by Toc H.

Have you not heard about Him,
O my brothers ?
Do you not know about Him,
O my sisters ?

He was a carpenter.
The wood yielded to His hands.
His yokes were easy upon the ox's neck,
and sweat was upon his brow.
He called Himself the Son of Man.
He did not despise the devadasi.
He cared for the beggar and the dog
that licked the beggar's sores.
He brought sight to the blind
and healed the leper.
He cured the diseased in mind
and gave them new life . . .

He gives a dream that will not
let a young man sleep.
He gives an adventure that will not
let a young man rest   . . .

He can give you life that is as bread
to your hungry bellies.
Listen to Him, O babu, toiling in your office.
He can give you life that is as hours
spent away from your desk.

Listen to Him, O men and women of India,
you and your children.
The hands that are His
will speed the plow through our fields of poverty.
The minds that are His
will create the plan which hums
in the roar of the city,
which throbs in the rhythm of the tabla
beaten in the village.
The hearts that are His
will clear the way and build the
road that is gentle even to crippled feet.
Let Him lead us in the march of Humanity,
to the wonder that awaits,
to the eye-unseen, the ear-unheard Future
that leads over star-track and Beyond!

Christ of the Indian Road: Chandran Devanesen, India.

Glory to Jesus the Lord
the Christ
the Saviour
the Son of God
the Son of Mary
The Man-God
the True Master
the True Person.

The Holy Eucharist: Forms of Worship
Jyotiniketan Ashram.

The transfiguration of our Lord:

O Lord, who art the ally and the aid of the young, we thank thee that thou hast called us at the outset of our life to follow thee; grant that we may dedicate our youthful powers to thy service, and fixing our gaze on thy shining countenance, may dutifully and faithfully serve thee to the end of our days: and this we ask of thy divine love. Amen.

Prayer used by Christian youth group in Shiraz, Iran.

The Triumphal Entry:

Jesus, King of the universe;
ride on in humble majesty,
ride on through conflict and debate,
ride on through sweaty prayer and betrayal of friends,
ride on through mockery and unjust condemnation,
ride on through cruel suffering and ignoble death,
ride on to the empty tomb and your rising in triumph,
ride on to raise up your Church, a new body for your service,
ride on, King Jesus, to renew the whole earth in your image;
in compassion come to help us. Amen.

Prayer used in Andhra Theological College, Hyderabad.

The Last Supper:

Har uzuma ya	In the chill of the spring evening
Pan saki tamo	The blessed Hands seem thin
Mi-te no yase.	As they break the bread.

Haiku: Tetsuzo Takeda, Japan.

Be present, be present, O Lord Jesus, thou good High Priest, as thou wast in the midst of thy disciples, and make thyself known to us in the breaking of the bread, who livest and reignest with the Father and the Holy Spirit, one God, world without end. Amen.

The Prayer of the Presence: Church of South India.

It remains to me a mystery.
This morning I knelt down to partake of the Holy elements.
I ate and drank the Holy bread and the Holy wine.
In my eating and drinking,
He ate me and drank me,
He is the food that eats the eater of the food.
I had the satisfaction that I had received the Lord.
But in my receiving Him,
It is He who received me.
He captured me and made me His.
It remains a mystery to me.

The food that eats: Meditation of an Indian
Christian.

The Passion:

Hast thou ever seen the Lord, Christ the Crucified?
Hast thou seen those wounded hands? Hast thou seen
His side?

Hast thou seen the cruel thorns woven for his crown?
Hast thou, hast thou seen His blood, dropping, dropping
down?

Hast thou seen who that one is who has hurt Him so?
Hast thou seen the sinner, cause of all His woe?

Hast thou seen how He, to save, suffers thus and dies?
Hast thou seen on whom He looks with his loving eyes?

Hast thou ever, ever seen love that was like this?
Hast thou given up thy life wholly to be his?

Narayan Vaman Tilak, India.

Wakakusa ya   The Cross drags heavily,
Jujika wa omuku   Tearing the earth
Chi ni hikare.   And its young grasses.

Haiku: Tetsuzo Takeda, Japan.

The earth's myriad forms our eyes now behold;
Their source the one God, Creator's sure hand.
No abstract void he, but the true living God:
One substance, three Persons, the Trinity blessed.

72

Our first parents' sin barred heav'n's open door,
But God's holy Son has shown us the way.
Man's sin he abolished, wiped out all our dread.
All rev'rence be given to him, truly-wise.

His work on the cross, completed: his blood,
A strong-flowing stream, brings grace to mankind.
Ere twice the cock crew, Peter thrice did deny.
Four times in the night he in judgement was tried.

Five thousand harsh strokes are but passing pain.
His six feet of flesh, two thieves hangs between.
His seven words ended, the spirits do sigh.
Earth's eight regions quake; the nine ranks stand aghast.

Ancient Chinese hymn, probably Nestorian.

O Tree of Calvary,
send your roots deep down
into my heart.
Gather together the soil of my heart,
the sands of my fickleness,
the mud of my desires.
Bind them all together,
O Tree of Calvary,
interlace them with Thy strong roots,
entwine them with the network
of Thy love.

Prayer of an Indian Christian.

I *hear*
The grinding,
Grinding,
As they take my leg;
I *see*
The Christ upon His Cross!

Prayer of Shinja: A Japanese leprosy patient.

In the blood-drops dripping
along the sorrowful road to the Via Dolorosa
will be written the history of man's regeneration.
Tracing those blood-stained and staggering footprints
let me go forward!
This day also must my blood flow, following
in that blood-stained pattern.

Toyohiko Kagawa, Japan.

73

Go-junan no
Seisho no ichiji
Ikku ka na.

From Holy Scripture
One word, one phrase recalled,
and all His agony reappears.

Haiku: Tetsuzo Takeda, Japan.

Just that
just that to say
very quiet, very soft
very gentle
in loneliness, in pain, in agony,
in terror, in fright,
just that remains in sleep and in dreams
in sorrow and in joy
one thing sweet remains
Christ never denying Himself.

Janet Rwagize: Uganda.

Resurrection:

Almighty God, who to thy holy Apostle Saint Thomas our
Patron didst reveal thine incarnate Son in his risen glory;
draw, we beseech thee, the peoples of our land to know
and confess him as their Lord and God, that coming to thee
by him they may believe and have life in his name;
through the same thy Son Christ our Lord and Saviour.

Amen.

*CIPBC Book of Common Prayer: Saint
Thomas the Apostle, Patron of India.*

Ah, the fragrance of new grass!
I hear His footsteps coming—
The Lord of the Resurrection!

*The Rt. Rev. M. Jiro Sasaki, formerly Bishop
of Kyoto; translation by Margaret Hisamatsu.*

Our Father, we come into the season of Easter, resolved . . .
to discipline our energies to clear goals,
to husband our time for reflection,
to school our tongues for praise,
and to soften our hearts for the acceptance of
wisdom, and, if necessary, for foolishness. Amen.

Prayer from Hawaii.

74

Pentecost:

Let your Spirit Break in

On your last days on earth
you promised
to leave us the Holy Spirit
as our present comforter.
We also know
that your Holy Spirit blows over this earth.
But we do not understand him.
Many think
he is only wind or a feeling.
Let your Holy Spirit
break into our lives.
Let him come like blood into our veins,
so that we will be driven
entirely by your will.
Let your Spirit
blow over wealthy Europe and America,
so that men there will be humble.
Let him blow over the poor parts of the world,
so that men there need suffer no more.
Let him blow over Africa,
so that men here may understand
what true freedom is.
There are a thousand voices and spirits
in this world,
but we want to hear only your voice,
and be open only to your Spirit. Amen.

Prayer of young Ghanaian Christian.

O God, who, when thou didst send down thy Spirit upon
thine Apostles, didst cause inhabitants of Iran to witness
that great event, and to believe: grant that we, the Persians
of today, finding strength and comfort from the Holy Ghost,
may be active and successful in the tasks of thy spiritual
Kingdom, through Jesus Christ our Lord. Amen.

Additional collect for Whitsunday, Iran.

O God, who to an expectant and united Church didst grant
at Pentecost the gift of the Holy Spirit, and hast wonderfully brought into one fold those who now worship thee
here; Grant, we beseech thee, the help of the same Spirit
in all our life and worship, that we may expect great
things from thee, and attempt great things for thee, and
being one in thee may show to the world that thou didst
send Jesus Christ our Lord, to whom with thee and the
Holy Spirit, be all honour and glory, world without end.
Amen.

The Book of Common Worship: The Church of South India.

PRAYERS OF THE CITY

May the Eternal God bless this city,
guard it against all evil,
guide it in wisdom.

May he bless all who build the Bridge,
and keep them faithful and safe in their work.

May the peoples of this city be united and godfearing,
happy and prosperous
preserving the good heritage of the past,
and building the future on foundations of
righteousness and love.

And all glory be to the Eternal God,
the Lord of the Worlds,
the Compassionate and Merciful,
the Ruler in History
and the lover of men,
the God and Father of Jesus Christ,
for ever and ever.   Amen.

Blessing composed by the Archbishop in
Jerusalem and pronounced by Brian de Saram
as Provost of Cairo, on the Cathedral steps
and looking out over the Nile, All Saints
Day, 1972.

" He cannot save Himself "—
Long ago
The crowds
Reviled a Man
Who came
To save them.

And I,
Who fain would follow Him,
Am spent.
For I can see
No hope
For the slums
Because that,
First of all,
This thing
Is wrong—

That men
Should crowd
Thus in the dearth,
And dark,
And dirt—
Should crowd and throng . . .
But oh,
The pity, the pity!
My people
Must stay
In the city;
So this six-foot shack
That shelters me
Is the only place
Where I want to be.

Songs from the Slums: Toyohiko Kagawa,
Japan.

Christ look upon us in this city,
And keep our sympathy and pity
Fresh, and our faces heavenward
Lest we grow hard.

Thomas Ashe, and found in St. Thomas'
clinic, Hong Kong.

O mighty and merciful God,
my family
prays to You,
glorifies and praises You,
adores You and pleads with You.
Here stands this small circle
before Your great majesty.
We would not dare pray to You
if Jesus had not said it was all right.

Lord of lords,
we put ourselves
under Your commands.
Most of our family is still in the village.
We are alone here in the city
and do not feel at home yet.
Many temptations and constant danger
surround us.
Lord,
please watch over these little children
when they go to school.
Those trucks and taxis go much too fast.

Lord, in this big city
without friends
we have only You to trust in.
We are afraid to be without a job—
and of death.
Lord,
protect us in this city.
We are at home wherever You are.
Stay with us, we pray.
Amen.

Prayer of Ghanaian Christian.

O Eternal Lord God, Source of all truth, Lover of all men,
we thank thee for the experience of living in this city.

Grant that we may be humble, grateful people,
worshipping people,
holy people.
Help us to be peace-loving people,
who know the things that belong to peace,
who pray and work for peace,
who try to understand the experiences, the
hurts, the hopes of people from whom we differ.
Let this city be a centre of unity for the Churches.
Let it be a place of friendship and understanding
for men of different faiths.
Let it be truly the City of Peace, a joy of the
whole earth and a place of blessing to all nations.
For the sake of him who wept in love over this
city and died in love outside its walls.
Now the Everlasting One, ever present with thee
to heal and bless, Jesus Christ our blessed Lord and Saviour.

George Appleton: prayed in Jerusalem.

O ye Jerusalem
Ten measures of beauty came into the world
Jerusalem took nine and the rest of the world one.
There are ten measures of suffering in the world
Nine in Jerusalem and one in the rest of the world.

*Quotation from the Jewish Sages, framed in
the entrance to an orphanage in East Jerusalem.*

O Jerusalem, Jerusalem . . .

Lord, dear Lord,
I long for Jerusalem:
The city built high in heaven
but also the one built on the rocks
over there in Irsael.

Lord,
neither London nor Paris
nor Moscow nor New York
entices me,
I long for Jerusalem.

How I would like to see Bethlehem
from far away in the fields
where the shepherds were,
go to the manger with them
and worship,
the smell of the animals around us,
the shepherds playing the flute
and I the drum.

Lord,
I would take Mary, Joseph and the Child
safely to Africa;
on hidden roads
not known to Herod
nor to the foreign power.

Lord,
in the midst of this ancient land
I would experience the wedding at Cana
and the wedding guests
happy with the wine
that Your Son,
the master of ceremonies, provided.
I would sit at Jacob's well,
dreaming of the ladder
that leads into heaven.
I would sit by the Sea of Galilee
and quietly say
the Sermon on the Mount,
and relive the miracle
of food for five thousand.

Then would I go up the hill to Jerusalem
rejoicing with the King of Glory.
Lord,
I would stand in front of Pilate's palace and shout:
" Let this one go;
He is innocent.
Take Barabbas,
Barabbas or—better—no one at all. "

Lord,
then I would see, in my mind,
how He was pushed and lashed
through city streets to Golgotha
and see there how He died for us.
I'd mourn and weep
and mourn—but I would know!
I'd see how the temple curtain was torn,
and feel the earthquake under my feet.
Then Easter.
when He rose from the dead.
Rejoicing, dancing and clapping
I would shout:
He is risen!
He is risen!
Lord,
I would like to see Jerusalem,
walk over the land where Jesus walked,
see all the villages,
the places where He preached
and performed His miracles.
Jesus of Nazareth,
Christ from Eternity.

Lord,
let me see this Jerusalem here on earth
and the one in heaven,
Amen.

On to Jerusalem: Prayer of Ghanaian Christian.

PRAYERS FOR UNITY

O God, who hast made of one blood
all nations of men
for to dwell on the face of the earth,
and didst send thy blessed Son Jesus Christ
to preach peace to them that are afar off,
and to them that are nigh:
Grant that all the peoples of this land
may feel after thee and find thee;
and hasten, O Lord,
the fulfilment of thy promise
to pour out thy Spirit
upon all flesh;
through Jesus Christ our Lord.

Bishop Cotton: Prayer for India.

We offer our thanks to Thee
for sending thy only Son to die for us all.
In a world suffocated with colour bars,
how sweet a thing it is to know
that in thee we all belong to one family.
There are times when we,
unprivileged people,
weep tears that are not loud but deep,
when we think of the suffering we experience.

We come to thee, our only hope and refuge.
Help us, O God, to refuse to be embittered
against those who handle us with harshness.
We are grateful to thee
for the gift of laughter at all times.
Save us from hatred of those who oppress us.
May we follow the spirit of thy Son Jesus Christ.

Prayer of an African pastor.

O God our Father, whose blessed Son came to bring unity
and fellowship among all men through his sacrifice on the
cross, hear us, we beseech thee today, as we pray for the
unity and peace of all the peoples and tribes of our country
of Uganda.

Forgive our past distrust and quarrels and rescue us from
the present evils of disunity.

Give special grace and wisdom at this time to the Rulers
and Councillors in the Protectorate, in the Kingdoms, in the
districts of Uganda, and to all leaders of the political
parties, that they may understand each other's points of
view and lead the peoples in co-operation, wisely and
strongly so that each tribe may preserve its good traditions
and each may make a proper contribution for a just
government for the whole country.

Leave us not desolate O God, but send unto us thy Holy
Spirit to strengthen and guide us into all truth; through
Jesus Christ, thy Son, our Lord.

Prayer for unity among the people of Uganda,
as appointed to be used in all churches in
Bukedi and Bugisu.

Our Father, to whom we give many names yet who are
One, bless the life of our islands, that as a variegated people
we shall yet remain as one in tolerance, respect, and aloha.
Keep us forever as peoples who have many ways, colours,
and histories bound together because we know that thou
didst intend us to live as a family.   Amen.

Prayer from Hawaii.

O God, who makest men to be of one mind in a house and
hast called us into the fellowship of thy dear Son; draw
into closer unity, we beseech thee, the people of all races
in this and every land; that in fellowship with thee they may
understand and help one another, and that, serving thee,
they may find their perfect freedom; through the same thy
Son, Jesus Christ our Lord.

Prayer suggested for use in South Africa.

O Lord, my Liege, unite us all!

Prayer of an old Muslim man overcome by
the grandeur of the Islamic Summit, Lahore 1974.

O God, we thank thee that thou hast brought us into the
fellowship of thy beloved Son Jesus Christ, that thou
mightest bind us into one.   We pray, O Lord, that people of
all races and tribes in this land and in every land may be led
into ways of co-operation and mutual understanding;
help them to work together in thee that they may be able to
help each other to find true freedom in serving thee;
through Jesus Christ our Lord.

From an order of Morning Prayer for
Independence of Uganda.

O God, thou art the loving Father of all the people in our
village, binding us together into one Great Family. Help
us to carry on all our relationships and our occupations,
crafts, trade and business for the welfare of the Great
Family, and not in the interests our of own selves, our own
families or our own groups.

Our family extends into the villages to which we have given
our daughters in marriage, and the villages from which we
have brought brides for our sons. It extends to towns to
which our children have gone for education, and our men
for work. It even extends to places in our country and the
world, which by travel, communications and mutual
dependence are knit together as one humanity.

In this family may we all be brothers and sisters without
caste or untouchability, without colour or race, but bound
together with love and concern for the whole great Family.
Gram Shri Niketan, Medak Diocese, Church of South India.

O God Thou art one—make us one.
Prayer used in India, though exact source unknown.

O God forgive us for bringing this stumbling block of
disunity to a people who want to belong to one family.
The Church for which our Saviour died is broken, and men
can scarcely believe we hold one Faith and follow one Lord.
O God bring about the union which thou hast commenced,
not tomorrow or the next day, but today.
A Prayer of an African minister.

O Lord, forgive the sins of thy servants. May we banish
from our minds all disunion and strife; may our souls be
cleansed from all hatred and malice towards others and
may we receive the fellowship of the Holy Meal in oneness
of mind and peace with one another.
*The Book of Common Worship, CSI
Supplement: Family Prayers.*

Vouchsafe, we beseech thee, Almighty God, to grant to the
whole Christian people unity, peace and true concord, both
visible and invisible, through Jesus Christ our Lord.
South African Prayer Book.

O Lord Jesus, stretch forth thy wounded hands
in blessing over thy people, to heal and to
restore, and to draw them to thyself and to
one another in love. Amen.
Prayer for the peoples of the Middle East.

Lord,
Your churches are quarrelling
among themselves.
Bishops are full of arrogance
and pretend
to be supermen.

Lord,
their traditions came to us
from Europe and America,
and also their great knowledge.
We do not understand their divisions.
We would like to be one church.

Lord,
Your Son prayed for one church!

Lord,
we pray for one church in Ghana,
one church in all of Africa.

Lord,
we are on our way to it;
give us so much love for our brothers
that all divisive thoughts
may be drowned in it.

Amen.

Prayer of a Ghanaian Christian.

Years ago in China there was a famous prayer: " Lord
revive thy Church—beginning with me. " This we can
alter slightly: " Lord unite thy Church beginning with me."

Church of North India suggestion for prayer.

Just as the bread which we break
Was scattered over the earth, was gathered in and became
one,
Bring us together from everywhere
Into the Kingdom of your peace.

Epistle to Diognetus.

PRAYERS OF DEDICATION

O Lord Jesus Christ, take out of our hearts unholy desires
and bad things; come into our hearts that we may be your
true servants and continue to worship you, and we may
learn and try to spread your way to our small and big
brothers.

Prayer of enquirer, Sind, Pakistan.

I saw the miracle the snow had wrought,
The white world shining silent here below,
And in my heart I prayed again to God,
' Lord, make me whiter, even, than the snow.'

Prayer of Nagata, Japanese leprosy patient.

From the cowardice that dare not face new truth
From the laziness that is contented with half truth
From the arrogance that thinks it knows all truth,
Good Lord, deliver me.

Prayer from Kenya.

Lord, I am afraid of my fear,
I am afraid of deserting Thee.
Lord, I am afraid of my fear,
I am afraid of not holding out right to the end.
Lord, I suffer, and I pray to Thee;
Glorious Thou art, forget me not.
The courage to give my life for Thee
Give Thou to me, and the love which will make me one
with Thee.

*Chinese Christian student after one of his
colleagues had apostasized, and then returned.*

Grant unto us thy servants
To our God—a heart of flame
To our fellow men—a heart of love
To ourselves—a heart of steel.

*A prayer adapted from St. Augustine of Hippo
and well known to past students of Bishop
Gwynne College, Mundri, Southern Sudan.*

Give me the supreme courage of love, this is my prayer—all courage to speak, to do, to suffer at thy will; to leave all or to be left alone.

Give me the supreme faith of love, this is my prayer—the faith of the life in death, of the victory in defeat, of the power hidden in the frailness of beauty, of the dignity of pain that accepts hurt but disdains to return it.   Amen.

Prayer of Rajkumari Kaur, India.

As the moon and its beams are one,
So, that I be one with Thee,
This is my prayer to Thee, my Lord,
This is my beggar's plea.

I would snare Thee and hold Thee ever
In loving, wifely ways;
I give Thee a daughter's welcome,
I give Thee a sister's praise.

Take Thou this body, O my Christ,
Dwell as its soul within.
To be an instant separate
I count a deadly sin.

Narayan Vaman Tilak: Christian poet of Maharashtra.

I ask to do Thy will in some humble, unambitious way,
O Lord, and to live a pure, bright, self-abandoned life.

Lord, I am willing to appear to the world and to all to have lost my life if I may only have made it good in Thy sight.

That I may come near to her, draw me nearer to Thee than to her; that I may know her, make me to know Thee more than her; that I may love her with the perfect love of a perfectly whole heart, cause me to love Thee more than her and most of all.   Amen. Amen.

That nothing may be between me and her, be Thou between us, every moment. That we may be constantly together, draw us into separate loneliness with Thyself. And when we meet breast to breast, my God, let it be on Thine own.   Amen.

Temple Gairdner of Cairo, before his marriage.

O Lord our Joy
May we love you more and more
Share in your caring for all
And lead some to your feet.

*Midday prayer of Women's Order of Sisters
and Companions for North India.*

O Lord Jesus, grant that my faith in thee may never fail,
but that it may continue to grow daily all through my life.
Bless my soul and my body, O Lord, that I may live in thee
and for thee till the end.   Amen.

O Almighty God, I humbly ask thee to make me like a tree
planted by the waterside, that I may bring forth fruits of good
living in due season.   Forgive my past offences, sanctify
me now, and direct all that I should be in the future; for
Christ's sake.   Amen.

Prayers used in Yoruba parishes in Nigeria.

Henceforth, let me burn out for God.   Amen.

Henry Martyn.

One day
I would like to take
Both my hands
(For I consider life itself too dear to lose)
Dip them in petrol
Then set them alight
With a candle flame
And dedicate them
To those who acted
While I wept and wrote.

Mahmood Jamal, Pakistan.

Doubly at thy service, O God.
                    Amen. Lord.

*Prayer used again and again by the Muslim
pilgrim during his period of consecration
at Mecca.*

I dedicate my life to God.
Take me, pardon me, polish me, keep me.
Use me O Lord, for the work thou wouldst give me to do.
When taking me, help me not to resist thee.

Prayer of a young African pastor included in
a letter.

Not for a rock cleft for me
not for insulation and bandaging
no, Lord
not for protection and paralysis
not for these do I pray.
I want to live
frustrated
and haunted
torn
crushed
grinded
in the machine of the breath.

No Lord
not for the warm bosom
not for the immaculate waters
not to be envied do I pray.
Care Lord
but in these murky puddles
in this scum allow me to stay
to taste " no rights "
and scream out
to embrace deprivation
and long
plead
clamour
and fight for more.

Lord for this I pray
that in this paradox
of tension and relief
of privilege and denial
of love and hatred
you may create heaven.

A prayer from Uganda: Godfrey Lubulwa.

That you are Lord to me,
suffices me for strength;
that I am servant to you,
suffices me for glory.

Arabic prayer of reliance.

O God, grant that always, at all times, and in all places, in
all things both small and great, we may ever do thy most
Holy Will and be Jesus Christ's faithful servants to our lives'
end.   Amen.

*Christa Sevika Sangha, Society of the
Servants of Christ, Bangladesh.*

Holy Spirit give us faith
Holy Spirit give us hope
Holy Spirit give us love
Revive thy work in this land beginning with me.

*Prayer used in Namirembe Diocese, Uganda,
during Lent.*

Men hate me for the curse I bear,
(I know it well)
But shall I heed them
Since my heart can be
A holy temple
Where my God can dwell?

Prayer of Handa, a Japanese leprosy patient.

O king of humility, whose abode is in the simple cottage of
a poor sweeper, help us to search for thee in this beautiful
land watered by the rivers Ganges, Yamuna and Brahmaputra.
Grant us an open and receptive heart, thy own humility,
power and longing to be one with the people of India.

O God, thou dost help man when he empties himself and
comes under thy protection. Grant us thy blessing that we
may never be separated from the people whom we serve as
their servants and friends. Make us embodiments of
sacrifice, devotion and humility, so that we may understand
our country better and love it the more.   Amen.

Prayer used in the Sarvodya Movement, India.

I am trusting Thee to get me out of ruts. To free my soul
that its whole power may go into moving forward; into
cloudless communion; into love; into effort.

Temple Gairdner's prayer during leave from Cairo.

O Lord, our palm trees can no longer hide us from the world.
Strengthen our hearts that we may look with confidence to
the future.

Prayer of an Tahitian pastor.

I am no longer my own, but thine. Put me to what thou
wilt, rank me with whom thou wilt; put me to doing, put
me to suffering; let me be employed for thee or laid aside
for thee, exalted for thee or brought low for thee; let me
be full, let me be empty; let me have all things, let me have
nothing; I freely and heartily yield all things to thy pleasure
and disposal.

And now, O glorious and blessed God, Father, Son, and
Holy Spirit, thou art mine, and I am thine. So be it. And
the covenant which I have made on earth, let it be ratified
in heaven.

*From the Covenant Service: The Book of
Common Worship, Church of South India.*

I take God the Father to be my God
        1 Thessalonians 1 : 9
I take Christ the Son to be my Saviour
        Acts 5 : 31
I take the Holy Spirit to be my Sanctifier
        1 Peter 1 : 2
I take the Word of God to be my rule
        2 Timothy 3 : 16, 17
I take the people of God to be my people
        Ruth 1 : 16, 17
I dedicate my whole self to the Lord *Romans 14 : 7, 8*
 and I do this deliberately   *Joshua 24 : 15*
  and sincerely   *2 Corinthians 1 : 12*
  and freely   *Psalm 110 : 3*
  and for ever.   *Romans 8 : 35–39*

*My Covenant. The Priest's Book of Private
Prayers, Bishop's College, Calcutta.*

PRAYERS OF SENDING

O God our Father it is to You that we plead endlessly for protection and safety when we travel. We come before you now, with our prayers for all drivers of motor vehicles, motorcycles and bicycles. Forgive us we pray for the heavy burden we lay upon You when we ask to be protected from the foolishness and carelessness of our fellowmen.

Teach those who drive, we pray, the spirit of humility and patience. May they realise that there is nothing to be gained from fast and careless driving except death and injury and heartache. Help us all to see that bad driving habits can turn a means of transport into a weapon of death and destruction as diabolical as the gun and the bomb. Hear us, O Lord when we call upon You for journey mercies. And help us to truly give thanks when we arrive at our destinations in safety.

Teach us all respect for the law, for the rules of the road, and for the rights of other road users. Help us to put our Christian faith into practice in the way that we drive so that we may set a good example.

Prayer suggested for use in the Diocese of Lagos, following the death of the elder son of a Nigerian clergyman in a motor accident.

To those who are travelling, good Lord, give a fair journey, whether by air or land or sea, by river, lake or road. Go with them in thy way, to give them back to their own people in happiness and health.

Prayer found in Karachi vicarage.

Go forth into the world in peace, looking up to Jesus, who was wounded for your transgressions, and bearing about in your lives the love and the joy and the peace, which are the marks of Jesus on his disciples; and so may the blessing of God, the Father, the Son and the Holy Spirit be upon you.

Blessing attributed to Canon Alipayo of Acholi.

91

Our Lord Jesus Christ send you forth in the power and
strength of the Holy Spirit to be his faithful witnesses to
your family, to your own country, and to the ends of the
earth.   *Prayer at end of Persian Confirmation service.*

Come, prepare us, for your Spirit, holy God we pray,
the Spirit with which you equipped your prophets, apostles,
martyrs, and confessors,
the Spirit who opens our hearts for your service as he did
their's.
We seek our brothers, and find them only when we open
our hearts to them.
We must speak your word to them aright.
They must understand that you are their Redeemer.
Otherwise they are lost.
Come, Holy Spirit,
prepare us to enter the huts of others.
                              The prayer of an African.

O Lord, thou art the king of our spirits.   Thou hast issued
orders to thy subjects to do a great work.   Thou hast
commanded them to preach the gospel to every creature.
We are going on that errand now.   Let thy presence go
with us to quicken us and enable us to persevere in the
great work until we die.
                    A Christian of the Hervey Islands.

O God, our Father, who does dwell in every place: may
thy everlasting arms defend our brethren who are about to
leave this home and go forth once more into the everyday
life of men. Grant them, we pray thee, courage and wisdom.
In all times of temptation or loneliness may thy strength and
joy fill their hearts.   Make them to show forth to others that
same spirit of compassion, which brought them healing
in this home, and lead them in the end to that eternal home
with thee, our Father, through Jesus Christ our Lord. Amen.
                    Prayer from Kumi Leprosy Centre, Uganda for
                                   those about to leave.

Hope is one of your best gifts to us.
Teach us to give it to others.
                              Exact source unknown.

Now may every living thing, young and old, weak and
strong, living near or far, known and unknown, living or
departed, or yet unborn, may every living thing be full of
bliss.

Buddhist aspiration: ' *There is in Buddhism*
a lovely devotional practice in which the
devout Buddhist sits in quiet meditation and
radiates to all living beings love, joy,
compassion and peace in turn.'

I am dumb,
dead,
tongue tied,
very dumb,
How can I communicate
so big a message?

How can pepper communicate the sweet,
how can failure radiate sucess?

The everlasting,
will it go with mud?

I am mud,
sticky mud.
Will I stick on the pure white?

But still
'' Go and preach ''
the Word tells me.
The drums and calabash,
the birds of the jungle
all cry
'' Go and preach
for God gave you power !''

Godfrey Lubulwa: Uganda.

O God our Father
And His Son Jesu Christ,
And the Holy Spirit,
May you give me a blessing while in this world,
While you lead me through the forests,
Through the lakes and the mountains,
So that I may do your work among your people,
Grant that I may be loved by you,
And by your people.   Amen.

This prayer, written in Luganda, was found
after the death of Apolo Kivebulaya on May
30, 1933, at the back of his pocket diary
for that year.

We are going home to many who cannot read.
So, Lord, make us to be Bibles
so that those who cannot read the Book
can read it in us.

Prayer of a Chinese woman after learning to read.

Strengthen, O Lord, the hands that holy things have taken,
that they may daily bring forth fruit to thy glory. Grant,
O Lord, that the lips which have sung Thy praise within the
sanctuary, may glorify Thee for ever; that the ears which
have heard the voice of Thy songs, may be closed to the
voice of clamour and dispute; that the eyes which have
seen Thy great love, may also behold Thy blessed hope;
that the tongues which have sung the Sanctus, may ever
speak the truth. Grant that the feet that have trod in
Thy holy courts may ever walk in the light, and that the
souls and bodies, which have tasted of Thy living Body and
Blood, may ever be restored in newness of life. Amen.

Liturgy of Malabar.

Reader:

Leave this chanting and singing and telling of beads!
Whom do you worship in this lonely dark corner of a temple
with doors all shut? Open your eyes and see your God
is not before you! He is where the tiller is tilling the hard
ground and where the pathmaker is breaking stones.
He is with them in sun and shower, and his garment is
covered with dust. Put off your holy mantle and even like
him come down on the dusty soil! Our master has joyfully
taken upon himself the bonds of creation; he is bound with
us all for ever. Come out of your meditations and leave
aside your flowers and incense! What harm is there if
your clothes become tattered and stained? Meet him and
stand by him in toil and in the sweat of your brow.

Rabindranath Tagore.

Leader:

Go forth into the world in peace; be of good courage;
hold fast that which is good; and the blessing of God
almighty, the Father, the Son, and the Holy Spirit, be upon
us and remain with us for ever.

Act of Commissioning, Dasara Service, as
used in United Theological College, Bangalore.

94

O Jesus
Be the canoe that holds me in the sea of life.
Be the steer that keeps me on the straight road.
Be the outrigger that supports me in times of great
temptation.
Let thy spirit be my sail that carries me through each day.
Keep my body strong,
so that I can paddle steadfastly on,
in the long voyage of life.   Amen.

A New Hebridean prayer.

Others delight in length
of days;
but I—
I wait for the lover that I
long for,
Death!

Prayer of Shirano, a Japanese leprosy patient.

O God, who hast in Thy love kept me vigorously and joyfully
at work in days gone by, and dost now send me joyful and
contented into silence and inactivity; grant me to find
happiness in Thee in all my solitary and quiet hours.   In Thy
strength, O God, I bid farewell to all.   The past Thou
knowest; I leave it at Thy feet.   Grant me grace to respond
to Thy Divine call; to leave all that is dear on earth, and go
out alone to Thee.   Behold, I come quickly, saith the Lord.
Come, Lord Jesus.

A prayer of a priest in old age: Premananda
Anath Nath Sen.

PRAYERS OF EVENING

The other evening as the whole family watched the sun go
down over the magnificent mountainous skyline across from
Suva harbour, " Just think, " said my wife, " as that sun is
sinking here behind those hills it is rising in England. "
That seemed a parable, somehow, of the presence of the
Lord with us always, binding his people together across the
world.

A missionary writing from Fiji.

Thick are the branches,
Forming a tent;
Velvety lawn
Is the altar;
The merciful moon,
Piercing through the foliage,
Shines on the ardent and peaceful face.

All is silent.
In the still and soundless air,
I fervently bow
To my almighty God.

Pray, weave the thread of your moonlight
Into my intellectual attire,
And a glorious crown,
That I can wear them
To face the world with softness and sweetness.

Hardship and vexation
Under your loving light
Are all thrown away;
I will strengthen myself, guide myself,
Forever in your presence,
Be a maiden pure,
And angel bright,
To glorify the Holy Spirit.

Hsieh Ping-Hsin: China.

The red sun dips into the shining sea
And marks the ending of the winter days;
Along the land the calm of evening steals,
While all my heart is lifted up in praise.

Prayer of Nagata, a Japanese leprosy patient.

My God and my Lord, eyes are at rest, stars are setting,
hushed are the movements of birds in their nests, of monsters
in the deep. And thou art the just who knowest no change,
the equity that swerveth not, the everlasting that passeth
not away. The doors are locked, watched by their
bodyguards. But thy love is open to him who calls on
thee. My Lord, each lover is now alone with his beloved.
Thou for me art the beloved One.

Abd Al-' Azuz Al-Dirini: Purity of Heart.

Whatever work seemed beautiful we did it all by the grace
of God.

*From an inscription in Persian cuneiform, four times
inscribed on the Propylaea at Persepolis, and carved on a
stone tablet behind the pulpit in the Church of Saint Simon
the Zealot, Shiraz, Iran. The words are by Xerxes and refer
to his palace.*

The long day has worn out my body
I give thanks
that I was able to work hard
for a good cause—
and that I earned some money.

Thanks,
Lord,
that I could use my voice,
my shoulders,
my arms,
my hands.

Lord,
I am tired,
I am falling asleep,
Hallelujah for this day!

Prayer of a young Ghanaian Christian.

We thank thee for the benediction of night, when the eye
no longer seeth, the ear no longer heareth and the mind
no longer thinketh. In that condition of night is all mankind
completely under thy rule. Lord let thy Holy Spirit go to
work on us tonight so that when the dawn comes our eyes
may see aright, our ears may hear aright, and our minds
may think aright.   *Prayer of an Asian Christian.*

Come,
Lord,
and cover me with the night.
Spread your grace over us
as you assured us you would do.

Your promises are more
than all the stars in the sky;
your mercy is deeper than the night.
Lord,
it will be cold.
The night comes with its breath of death.
Night comes,
the end comes,
but Jesus Christ comes also.

Lord,
we wait for him
day and night.
Amen.
                          Prayer of a young Ghanaian Christian.

When our factories have turned out their last products,
When our business men have made their last deals,
When the last tired clerk is dismissed,
When the banks have raked in the last Naira,
When the judge of the earth says: ' Close for the night '
and asks for balance—what then?

When the choir has sung its last anthem
And the preacher has said his last prayer,
When the people have heard their last sermon,
And the sound has died out on the air,
When the Bible lies closed on the pulpit,
And the pews are all empty of men,
When each one stands facing his record,
And the great book is opened—what then?

When in the All Africa games
All the nations have marched past the stand,
The last athlete has breasted the tape,
And the crowds have finished their cheering,
When the multi-million Naira stadium is deserted
And the busy streets of Lagos are calm
And the world that rejected its Saviour
is asked for a reason—what then?

When the commander's last call sinks in silence
And the long marching columns stand still,
When the company has captured its target,
And the victory flag has been raised,
When the trump of the ages is sounded
And we stand up before Him—what then?
What then? What then? What then? What then
will you achieve when this life's race is ended?

What then? Chukwu Ogbajie, Nigeria.

O Lord, Creator,
Ruler of the world, Father,
I thank, thank, thank you
that you have brought me through.
How strong the pain was—
but you were stronger.
How deep the fall was—
but you were even deeper.

How dark was the night—
but you were the noonday sun in it.
You are our father,
our mother,
our brother, and our friend.
Your grace has no end,
and your light no snuffer.
We praise you,
we honour you,
and we pray to your holy name.
We thank you
that you rule thus,
and that you are so merciful
with your tired followers.
Praise be to you
through our Lord Jesus Christ.
Amen.

You are like the noonday sun in the night:
Prayer of a Ghanaian Christian.

All that we ought to have thought, and have not thought,
All that we ought to have said, and have not said,
All that we ought to have done, and have not done;

All that we ought not have thought, and yet have thought,
All that we ought not to have spoken, and yet have spoken,
All that we ought not to have done, and yet have done;
For thoughts, words and works, pray we, O God, for
forgiveness.

From an ancient Persian prayer.

I kneel, O Lord,
To pray to Thee,
And do not know
When the hot tears
That wet my cheeks
Begin to flow!

Shirano: Prayer of a Japanese leprosy patient.

O Thou great Chief, light a candle in my heart, that I may
see what is therein, and sweep the rubbish from thy
dwelling place.

An African schoolgirl's prayer.

O Peaceful King of Peace, Jesus Christ, give unto us thy
peace, and confirm unto us thy peace, and forgive us our
sins, so that we may be worthy to come and go in peace.

Ethiopian Liturgy.

Our Father in heaven, we thank thee for the good things
thou givest us day by day; for food and medicine, for our
homes and children, and thou givest us all things.   But we
do not understand thy word enough yet, and we are not so
faithful to thee as thou wouldst have us be.   Forgive us our
sins and take them from us.   Teach us the word of thy
Son Jesus Christ, that we may put it in our hearts and follow
him; and watch over us all now and always, for we ask
these things in Jesus' name.

A prayer of Katcha origin: prayer for forgiveness.

Evening came wandering slowly
into our shadow-haunted mango grove
like some old rishi come to worship.
Silence dripped from the quietened leaves
and every blade of grass was still.
Overhead crowds of attendant clouds
were trimming the lamps of heaven.
The sky drew closer to the earth
to hush it to sleep.
Looking at the vast expanse above
I remembered how the ancients
on the plains of Aryavarta
had called it Om.

Om! Our lips scarce form the word
ere it speeds forth, vibrant as an arrow,
and goes winging past the stars
to the uttermost boundaries of the universe.

Om! one mystic syllable
that sends the mind rippling across pools of space,
along endlessly reverberant tracks of sound
that leads to the mouth of God.

Thoughts from the sky: Prayer/poem of an Indian
Christian.

You are much stronger than Juju

You know, dear God,
my people still believe much in juju.
But I don't believe in it any more,
since I believe in you.
But sometimes
I am afraid of it.
Now they are trying again
to get at me with juju.
They want to put
something bad in my head.
They believe in it.
They drum for it,
they dance for it,
and they sing for it.
And I can do nothing about it.
I don't believe in it any more
but I am still afraid of it.
You are much stronger than juju.
Halleluja, Halleluja,
you are my God,
mine, mine, mine.

My great God,
great, great, great.
My strong God,
strong, strong, strong.
My loving God,
loving, loving, loving.
My redeemer, my saviour.
my father, father, father.
My hut,
my shadow,
my redeemer, my redeemer, my redeemer.
You are my cave.
my door and my weapon,
when now
evil ones are making juju against me.
But you are still stronger,
much much stronger.
They are dancing around the drums.
They are making juju against me.
But I will depend entirely on you.
I can do nothing against this juju.
I won't get another fetish priest.
I'll depend only on you.
Even when I am sick
I won't get a fetish priest.
Yes, I have you.
You are always there.
I depend on you.
I thank, thank, thank you.
What is juju against you?
Juju can do nothing
where you are.
Amen.

Prayer of a Ghanaian Christian.

Merciful and holy God, lead us not into temptation to see
evil in others, but deliver us from evil in each one of us, so
that we may love our neighbour even when we believe he
is a witch.

Especially open our eyes for what thou wouldest say to us
through need, suffering, sorrow and illness so that all this
may draw us to thee and not away from thee.

Deliver us from the anxiety of life and the anxiety of death, deliver us from the fear of witches, and renew a steadfast spirit within us, thou Holy Spirit of discipline.

To be prayed with an African brother or sister living under the fear of witchcraft.

May the Cross of the Son of God who is mightier than all the hosts of Satan, and more glorious than all the angels of heaven abide with you in your going out and your coming in! By day and night, at morning and at evening, at all times and in all places, may it protect and defend you! From the wrath of evil men, from the assaults of evil spirits, from foes invisible, from the snares of the devil, from all low passions that beguile the soul and body, may it guard, protect, and deliver you.

The Christaraksha: Book of Common Prayer: Church of India, Pakistan, Burma and Ceylon.

The sun has disappeared.
I have switched off the light,
and my wife and children are asleep.
The animals in the forest are full of fear,
and so are the people on their mats.
They prefer the day with your sun
to the night.
But I still know that
your moon is there,
and your eyes
and also your hands.
Thus I am not afraid.
This day again
you led us wonderfully.
Everybody went to his mat
satisfied and full.
Renew us during our sleep,
that in the morning
we may come afresh to our daily jobs.
Be with our brothers far away in Asia
who may be getting up now.
Amen.

I am not afraid: Prayer of a young Ghanaian Christian.

ABOUT THE PRAYERS

Morning:

Toyohiko Kagawa, Meditations, *Kagawa,* William Axling, SCMP.

Thomas Merton: *Conjectures of a Guilty Bystander.*

Prayer attributed to John Hoyland: *The Priest's Book of Private Prayers.* Bishop's College, Calcutta.

Chandran Devanesen; *The Cross is Lifted,* Friendship Press, New York.

Prayer of Armenian Apostolic Church: *Children's Prayers from Other Lands.* D. Spicer.

Prayer by Miyoshi, a Japanese leprosy patient: *Escaped as a Bird.* Leprosy Mission.

Meditations of an Indian Christian: M.A. Thomas, SCM.

Richard Wong: *Prayers from an island,* John Knox Press, Richmond, Virginia.

Prayer of Egyptian Coptic Church, *Children's Prayers from Other Lands.* D. Spicer.

Rt. Rev. Kimber H. K. Den, Bishop of Chekiang.

For fitness to be guests at God's banquet: *A Book of Prayers written for use in an Indian college,* author unknown.

Prayer by Nagata, a Japanese leprosy patient: *Escaped as a Bird.*

Richard Wong; *Prayers from an island.*

Original source of prayer unknown: *The Priest's Book of Private Prayers.* Bishop's College, Calcutta.

Narayan Vaman Tilak: The Christian Poet of Maharashtra, J. C. Winslow, SCM., 1923, and *From Brahma to Christ* by L. Tilak, World Christian Books, 1956.

M. A. Thomas: *Meditations of an Indian Christian, SCM.*

Prayer used by Companions of Brother Lawrence, India.

A Prayer sometimes used by members of the Christa Mahila Sadan, Women's Centre, North India.

Prayers of Presence:

T. K. Thomas, Editorial Secretary of Christian Literature Society, Madras.

James Michener: *Tales of the South Pacific.*

Worship in Youth's Idiom. Ecumenical Christian Centre, Bangalore.

Prayer by Utsunomiya, a Japanese leprosy patient: *Escaped as a Bird.*

Prayer of Ibn-al-Arabi. The reader's attention is especially drawn to Kenneth Cragg's compilation of Muslim and Christian prayer, with introductory essay: *Alive to God,* OUP.

Well-known Jewish prayer. Other prayers from Jewish and many other sources will be found in: *God of a Hundred Names,* Gollancz.

Sa'adi, Persian poet, 15th century.
Prayer of Xhosa Christian: *In His Name,* George Appleton, EHP.
Prayer of Narayan Vaman Tilak.
The Trisagion, *The Liturgy of the Church of South India,* Christian Literature Society, Madras.
Chinese Trinitarian formula, used in the worship of the Nestorian Church: *The Cross and the Lotus,* Lee Shiu Keung, Christian Study Centre on Chinese Religion and Culture.
Prayer of Dadu, 16th Century Hindu poet and mystic.
Well-known prayer of St. Augustine of Hippo. 354–430 AD.
Prayer ascribed to the oral tradition of a hill tribe in Northern Bengal.
Prayer of Ramanuja, page 29 of Introduction, *The Upanishads,* translated by Juan Mascaró, Penguin Classics, 1965.
Reprinted by permission of Penguin Books Ltd.
Prayer of Chaitanya, the Indian mystic of AD 1500, page 33 of Introduction, *The Upanishads,* Penguin Classics.
Prayer of Companions of Brother Lawrence, India.
M.A. Thomas, A garland: *Meditations of an Indian Christian,* SCM.

Prayers of need:

Toyohiko Kagawa: *Meditations.*
M. A. Thomas, I wept for love: *Meditations of an Indian Christian,* SCM.
An African's prayer: exact source unknown.
Prayer by Yamagata, a Japanese leprosy patient, *Escaped as a Bird.*
Prayer of Sadhu Sundar Singh: *The Gospel of Sadhu Sundar Singh,* Friedrich Heiler, Lucknow Publishing House.
Prayer used by the Khonds in North India.
Prayer of Rabia of Jerusalem: *Journey for a Soul,* George Appleton, Fontana Books.
Prayer of Japanese Christian novelist and seeker, Rinzo Shiina, quoted in *Japan Christian Quarterly.*
A Muslim prayer, used after the Muslim pilgrim to Mecca has begun the seventh circuit of the Kabah. For other Muslim prayers the reader is referred to: *Muslim Devotions,* Constance Padwick, SPCK., and to: *Alive to God,* Kenneth Cragg, OUP.
Prayers of a Kenyan Christian, exact source unknown.
Tukutendereza prayer of forgiveness and praise translated into Luganda from the original English and used by Balokeli Christians in East Africa. *Breath of Life.* Patricia St. John, The Norfolk Press.
Lenten prayer as used in many Nigerian churches.
Prayer of United Church of North India.
Prayer used in diocese of Krishna-Godavari, Church of South India.

An African teacher's prayer: *In His Name,* George Appleton, EHP.
Prayer of 11 year-old child on hearing of Sino-Indian border fighting, exact source unknown.
Prayer of Akanu Ibiam, Nigeria.
Prayer from Africa: *African Features, 1961.*
George Appleton: *Jerusalem Prayers,* SPCK.
Inscription on tomb of Mumtaz Mahal, Agra.
Prayer of Uruguayan survivors of plane crash in the Andes: *Alive: the story of the Andes Survivors,* Piers Paul Read, Secker & Warburg.
Letter to God, Pakistani Muslim student.

Prayers of life and work:

Prayer Book of the Church of India, Pakistan, Burma and Ceylon.
Prayer used in the Medak Diocese, Church of South India: *Prayers for Village People,* S. P. Raju.
East African hymn used at Seed Consecration Service.
Prayer used by many Indian Christian farmers at the time of dedication of a threshing floor: *A Book of Worship for Village Churches,* Rural People at Worship, Agricultural Missions Inc.
Prayer for poor labouring folk: *Worship Resources from the Chinese,* Chao Tzu-Ch'en, 1931, arranged by Bliss Wiant, Friendship Press, New York.
A prayer of Zande Christians, Southern Sudan, source unknown.
Prayer for palm oil and coconut industries; *Book of Occasional Services,* Niger and Niger Delta dioceses.
Prayer for the market, source as above.
Truck driver's prayer: *I sing your praise all the day long: Young Africans at Prayer*, Ed. Fritz Pawelzik, Friendship Press, New York.
Short prayers for Christian women, Christian Homes Movement of China.
Service for Blessing of Canoes and Nets: *Book of Occasional Services,* Niger and Niger Delta dioceses.
Prayer used at Industrial Thanksgiving Service, Jinja Industrial Mission, Uganda.
Short prayers for Christian men, Christian Homes Movement of China.
Richard Wong: *Prayers from an Island*.
Emmanuel Twesigye: *Creative Moments*, Uganda Church Press.
Prayers from Wanyange Girls' School, Jinja, commemorating famous names and places.
Night over our school: *I sing your praise all the day long: Young Africans at Prayer.*

Prayers of compassion:

Toyohiko Kagawa: *Meditations.*
Worship in Youth's Idiom, Ecumenical Christian Centre, Bangalore.
Prayer of an African Christian, exact source unknown.
Daily prayer of Mother Teresa of Calcutta: *Something Beautiful for God,* Malcolm Muggeridge, Fontana Books.
Richard Wong: *Prayers from an Island.*
A prayer from Kenya for the hungry, from a Christian Council source.
Prayer based on the parable of the Good Samaritan as used in Hong Kong, and by Bishop R. O. Hall.
Exact source unknown, but used by Congregational Prayer Fellowship.

Prayers for much loved lands:

For India

Augustine Ralla Ram: *In His Name,* George Appleton, EHP.
Douglas Webster, written during a visit to India.
Day of Prayer for our country, National Christian Council of India source.
Narayan Vaman Tilak.

For Nepal

Prayer/hymn of Nepal Christians, prayed over many years on the borders of Nepal: *Nepal on the Potter's Wheel,* UMN.

For Pakistan

John Carden: *Empty Shoes,* Highway Press.

For Iran

Ancient prayer of Darius, inscribed these days on Shiraz Airport.
Henry Martyn prayer: *Brief description of the Church of Saint Simon the Zealot, Shiraz,* by Norman Sharp.

For Israel

George Appleton: *Jerusalem prayers,* SPCK.
Prayer used at Memorial Service in Jerusalem, and quoted by George Appleton.

For the Middle East

CMS source.
Exact source unknown.

For Hong Kong & Macao

Bishop R. O. Hall.

For Sabah

A Tongud Litany compiled by Sheila Merryweather, *Sabah Diocesan Magazine.*

For Japan
> Akira Ebisawa: *In His Name,* George Appleton, EHP.
> Toyohiko Kagawa.

For China
> Prayer of a Chinese Christian: *In His Name,* George
> Appleton, EHP.
> Bishop Charles Perry Scott's prayer for the Chung Hua
> Sheng Kung Hui, the Chinese Holy Catholic Church.

For Africa
> Bishop Huddleston's prayer for Africa.
> An African Canticle, *Maryknoll Magazine.*
> A prayer commended by the Christian Council of Nigeria.

Prayers for freedom:
> James Aggrey, The Parable of the Eagle: *Aggrey of Africa,*
> Edwin W. Smith, SCM.
> Daisuke Kitagawa, Department of Church and Society,
> WCC publication.
> George Appleton: *In His Name,* EHP.
> Chief Hosea Kutako, exact source unknown.
> Richard Wong: *Prayers from an Island.*
> Prayer of a West Indian Christian: *In His Name,* George
> Appleton, EHP.
> Adapted form of Rabindranath Tagore's prayer for true
> freedom; Worship for Independence Day, Andhra Christian
> Theological College, Hyderabad, *Services for all Seasons.*
> D. Appadurai. Cloud Cuckoo-Land: *Other Voices, Other
> Places:* An anthology of Third World Poetry, Christian Aid.
> Yasmin Abassi, Pakistan.
> Prayer of Hindu village girl in Orissa: *My Village, My Life,*
> Prafulla Mohanti, Davis Poynter, London.

Prayers of following:
> Prayer of the East Asia Christian Council Youth Consultation.
> Adapted from prayer prayed in Mengo Hospital, Uganda.
> Prayer of Mustafah the tailor: *Christian Homes of India,
> No. 51.*
> First audible prayer of Temple Gairdner: *Temple Gairdner
> of Cairo,* Constance Padwick, SPCK.
> Firoz Uddin, a Bengali Muslim follower of Jesus; source
> Allan Jenkins, CMS missionary in Calcutta.
> M. A. Thomas, I want to be lazy: *Meditations of an Indian
> Christian,* SCM.
> Prayer used at the CWME Assembly, Bangkok, 1973.
> Aspiration of Companions of Brother Lawrence, India.
> Robin Boyd: *United Church Review,* June, 1963.
> Darshan, Chandran Devanesen: *The Cross is Lifted.*
>> darshan: vision
>> sannyasi: religious mendicant
>> kirtans: lyrics
>> puja: worship, offering.

Prayer for missionaries:
> Fedrico Pagura, Methodist Bishop of Costa Rica.
> Brother Lewis is leaving us: *I sing your praise all the day long: Young Africans at prayer.*
> Prayer of Sudanese pastor, source unknown.
> Prayer offered in Malayalam by delegate to World Missionary Conference, Edinburgh, 1910.

The Third World claims a share in interpreting and commemorating the life of our Lord:

Advent:
> Chandran Devanesen, Advent: *The Cross is Lifted.*

The Nativity:
> Prayer by Ozaki, a Japanese leprosy patient: *Escaped as a Bird.*
> *The Book of Common Worship*, Church of South India.
> Narayan Vaman Tilak.
> Prayer suggested for use in the Lucknow Diocese, Church of North India.
> Father James Takeda, SSJE: *Father Tetsu's Collection of Haiku Poems.*

The Holy Innocents:
> Prayer of Archbishop Helder Camara of Brazil, *Church Times.*
> Prayer/poem of Simon Baynes, CMS missionary in Japan; *The Japan Christian Quarterly,* Summer 1973.

Flight into Egypt:
> Lenrie Peters, Gambian poet and novelist, quoted by Martin Jarrett-Kerr, Christian Faith and the African Imagination: *Christian,* Easter 1973.
> Bishop Kenneth Cragg: ' The sojourn in Egypt is a bit of history which means a great deal to the Coptic church and to Coptic evangelicals also. '

Epiphany:
> The Holy Eucharist: *Forms of Worship,* Jyotiniketan, Ashram, North India and Jerusalem.
> John Carden: *Empty Shoes.*
> Chandran Devanesen: *The Cross is Lifted.*
> Additional Collect for the Epiphany, Iran.
> *The Book of Common Worship:* CSI.
> Ancient Brihadaranyaka prayer, adapted for use in Andhra Christian Theological College ' In this way we have incorporated the important triadic concept of Sat-chit-ananda and related it to the Christian Trinitarian experience.

In other words, when we first respond to God's call, we begin with those aspirations lying deep in the Indian consciousness.'

A modern Shiraz poet, Hamidi, refers to the visit of the Persian Magi to our Lord in his infancy: *Brief Description of the Church of Saint Simon the Zealot, Shiraz, Iran,* by Norman Sharp.

The Holy Childhood:
Prayer used in daily worship at the Christukula Ashram in Tirappatur, South India.
Based on a story of the child Jesus in the Apocryphal Gospel of Thomas: source unknown.

The Ministry:
Personal prayer of Bishop Jacob, Bishop of Travancore, South India.
A Litany of the Disciples of the Servant: *Services for all Seasons from Andhra Christian Theological College, Hyderabad.* Carries the note: ' this may be led by a layman.'
Prayer used in the world-wide Toc H.
Chandran Devanesen, Christ of the Indian Road; *The Cross is Lifted.*
The Holy Eucharist: *Forms of Worship,* Jyotiniketan Ashram, North India and Jerusalem.

Transfiguration:
Prayer used by Christian youth group in Shiraz, Iran.

The Triumphal Entry:
Worship of the Servant Lord: *Services for all Seasons from Andhra Christian Theological College, Hyderabad.*

The Last Supper:
James Tetsuzo Takeda: Haiku.
The Prayer of the Presence: *Liturgy of the Church of South India.* The note reads: " Both parts of the prayer are very ancient. The first part comes from the offertory prayer of the Mozarabic Liturgy; and the second sentence from the *Teaching of the Apostles,* a second century work, from which we get one of the earliest accounts of the celebration of the Eucharist. This prayer links our action with the appearance of the Risen Christ to the two disciples at Emmaus when He was ' known to them in the breaking of bread'."
M. A. Thomas, The Food that eats: *Meditations of an Indian Christian.*

The Passion:

Narayan Vaman Tilak.

James Tetsuza Takeda: Haiku.

Bliss Wiant: *Worship Resources from the Chinese.* 'In this ancient hymn, possibly Nestorian, several interesting points emerge: (a) Insistence on a Creator God, as against the Buddhist concept of reality as the Void. (b) The stream of grace flowing from the West, for the hymn was written in China. (c) Number symbolism, in which Chinese scholars delighted (*six* feet—the Chinese estimate of the length of a man's body; *eight* regions, into which the earth was thought to be divided; *nine* ranks—official grades or ranks in ancient China).

Chandran Devanesen, Send your roots deep down: *The Cross is Lifted.*

Prayer by Shinja, a Japanese leprosy patient: *Escaped as a Bird.*

Toyohiko Kagawa.

James Tetsuzo Takeda: Haiku.

Janet Rwagize: *Creative Moments,* Uganda Church Press.

The Resurrection:

Collect for St. Thomas the Apostle, Patron of India: *CIPBC Book of Common Prayer.*

Rt. Rev. M. Jiro Sasaki, formerly Bishop of Kyoto; translated by Margaret Hisamatsu.

Richard Wong: *Prayers from an Island.*

Pentecost:

Let your Spirit Break in: *I Lie on My Mat and Pray: Prayers by Young Africans*, Friendship Press, New York.

Additional collect for Whitsunday, Iran.

Book of Common Worship: Church of South India.

Prayers of the city:

Prayer composed by George Appleton and pronounced by Provost of Cairo, All Saints Day, 1972.

Toyohiko Kagawa, *Songs from the Slums*.

Thomas Ashe.

Prayer for the city: *I sing your praise all the day long: Young Africans at Prayer.*

George Appleton: *Jerusalem Prayers,* SPCK.

Quotation from the Jewish Sages; *St. Luke 13. 34.*

On to Jerusalem: *I sing your praise all the day long: Young Africans at prayer.*

Prayers for unity:

Bishop Cotton Prayer for India: *Book of Common Prayer,* CIPBC.

Prayer of a Bantu pastor, exact source unknown.

Prayer for unity among the people of Uganda, source unknown.
Richard Wong: *Prayers from an island.*
Prayer suggested for use in South Africa.
Prayer of old Muslim man: *Pakistan Times, 1974.*
From an order of Morning Prayer for Independence of Uganda, 1962.
Prayer used in Medak Diocese, Church of South India: *Prayers for Village People,* S. P. Raju.
Prayer used in India, source unknown.
Prayer of an African minister, source unknown.
The Book of Common Worship, Supplement, Church of South India.
South African Prayer Book.
Prayer for unity in Middle East, exact source unknown.
I sing your praise all the day long: Young Africans at Prayer.
Church of North India: suggestion for prayer.
Epistle to Diognetus.

Prayers of dedication:

Prayer of enquirer, Sind, Pakistan, *Sind Newsletter, NZCMS.*
Prayer by Nagata, a Japanese Leprosy patient: *Escaped as a Bird.*
Prayer from Kenya, Christian Council source.
Prayer of Chinese Christian student. Jean Lefeuvre, Shanghai, *Les Enfants dans la ville.*
A prayer adapted from St. Augustine of Hippo, and well known to past students of Bishop Gwynne College, Mundri, S. Sudan.
Prayer of Rajkumari Kaur. From: *Prayers for a Busy Day.*
Narayan Vaman Tilak.
Temple Gairdner of Cairo, Constance Padwick, SPCK.
Midday prayer of Women's Order of Sisters and Companions, CNI.
Prayers used in Yoruba parishes in Nigeria.
Henry Martyn: Constance Padwick, 1923.
Mahmood Jamal, Pakistan. *Other Voices, Other Places:* An Anthology of Third World Poetry, Christian Aid.
Prayer of the Muslim pilgrim. For further prayers see *Muslim Devotions,* Constance Padwick, SPCK.
Prayer of young African pastor, exact source unknown.
Godfrey Lubulwa: *Creative Moments,* Uganda Church Press.
Arabic prayer of reliance, quoted by Kenneth Cragg.
Prayer of sisters of Christa Sevika Sangha, Society of the Servants of Christ, Bangladesh.
Prayer used in Namirembe Diocese, Uganda.
Prayer by Handa, a Japanese leprosy patient: *Escaped as a Bird.*
Prayer used in Sarvodya Movement, India.
Temple Gairdner of Cairo: Constance Padwick, SPCK.

Prayer of Tahitian pastor, exact source unknown.
The Covenant Service, *Book of Common Worship,* Church of South India.
The Priest's Book of Private Prayers; My Covenant.
Bishop's College, Calcutta.

Prayers of Sending:

Prayer suggested for use in Diocese of Lagos, *Lagos Diocesan Letter.*
Prayer found in Karachi vicarage.
Blessing attributed to Canon Alipayo of Acholi.
Prayer at conclusion of Persian Confirmation Service.
Prayer of an African, exact source unknown.
Prayer of Christian of the Hervey Islands.
Prayer from Kumi Leprosy Centre, Uganda.
Prayer for hope, source unknown,
Buddhist aspiration: *One Man's Prayers,* George Appleton, SPCK.
Godfrey Lubulwa: *Creative Moments,* Uganda Church Press.
Prayer of Canon Apolo Kivebulaya.
Prayer of Chinese woman: *In His Name,* George Appleton, EHP. According to Daniel J. Fleming: *The World at One in Prayer*—" After a four months ' refugee Bible class in which a number of illiterate women had learned to read, the day came when they were returning to their homes. At the meeting before parting one of the women used this prayer. " Liturgy of Malabar.
Rabindranath Tagore: *Gitanjali.*
Act of Commissioning from Dasara Celebration Service, UTC Bangalore.
A New Hebridean prayer, exact source unknown.
Prayer by Shirano, a Japanese leprosy patient: *Escaped as a Bird.*
Prayer of a priest in old age: *Premananda Anath Nath Sen Autobiography.* SPCK of India.

Prayers of Evening:

David and Wendy Williams, CMS missionaries, Suva, Fiji.
Hsieh Ping-Hsin: after Psalm 145, *Worship Resources from the Chinese,* Bliss Wiant.
Prayer of Nagata, a Japanese leprosy patient: *Escaped as a Bird.*
Abd Al–' Azuz Al–Dirini: *Purity of Heart.*
Inscription by Xerxes: *Brief Description of the Church of Saint Simon the Zealot, Shiraz, Iran,* by Norman Sharp.
I sing your praise all the day long: Young Africans at Prayer.
Prayer of an Asian Christian, exact source unknown.
I sing your praise all the day long: Young Africans at Prayer.

Chukwu Ogbajie, *What then?* Trinity Theological College magazine, Umuahia.

I lie on my mat and pray: Prayers by Young Africans. You are like the noonday sun in the night.

An ancient prayer, exact source unknown.

Prayer by Shirano, a Japanese leprosy patient: *Escaped as a Bird.*

An African schoolgirl's prayer: *God's Candlelights,* Mabel Shaw.

Prayer from the Ethiopian Liturgy.

An evening prayer for forgiveness, of Katcha origin.

Thoughts from the sky, Chandran Devanesen: *The Cross is Lifted.*

    rishi: ascetic hermit
    Om: a mystic syllable signifying divine reality.

You are much stronger than Juju; *I lie on my mat and pray: Prayers by Young Africans.*

A prayer to be used with an African brother or sister living under the fear of witchcraft, exact source unknown.

The Christaraksha: *Book of Common Prayer, Church of India, Pakistan, Burma and Ceylon.*

I am not afraid; *I lie on my mat and pray: Young Africans at Prayer.*

Our thanks are due to publishers and copyright owners for permission to use extracts from publications quoted in this book. Every effort has been made to trace the holders of copyrights and we apologise for any errors or omissions.